Dear Lama Zopa

ANSWERS TO LETTERS ON ANGER ANIMALS CHILDREN

DEATH DEPRESSION DIVORCE DREAMS DRUGS FAME

FEAR FORGIVENESS GOD GRIEF HEALING JEALOUSY

MONEY RELATIONSHIPS SUING VEGETARIANISM WAR

AND OTHER LIFE STRUGGLES

Dear Lama Zopa

Radical Solutions for Transforming Problems into Happiness

Illustrations and calligraphy by the author

Edited by Robina Courtin, with Diana Finnegan and
Michelle Bernard of Lama Yeshe Wisdom Archive

Wisdom Publications • Boston

Wisdom Publications
199 Elm Street
Somerville MA 02144 USA
wisdompubs.org

Library of·Congress Cataloging-in-Publication Data
Thubten Zopa, Rinpoche, 1946-
  Dear Lama Zopa : radical solutions for transforming problems into happiness / Lama
Zopa Rinpoche ; illustrations and calligraphy by the Lama Zopa Rinpoche ; edited by
Robina Courtin, with Diana Finnegan and Michelle Bernard of Lama Yeshe Wisdom
Archive.
     p. cm.
  ISBN 0-86171-289-7 (pbk. : alk. paper)
  1. Religious life—Buddhism. 2. Thubten Zopa, Rinpoche, 1946—Correspondence. I.
Courtin, Robina. II. Finnegan, Diana. III. Bernard, Michelle. IV. Title.
  BQ7775.T49 2007
  294.3'444—dc22
                         2007010095
  ISBN 0-86171-289-7

11 10 09 08 07
5   4   3   2   1

Designed by Arnoud Smits, Naropa Graphic Design | www.naropa.nl
Set in Minion Pro 11/14 and Avenir fonts.
Cover photograph by Ven. Roger Kunsang.

Wisdom Publications' books are printed on acid-free paper and meet the guidelines
for permanence and durability of the Committee on Production Guidelines for Book
Longevity of the Council on Library Resources.

Printed in the United States of America

This book was produced with environmental mindfulness. We have elected
to print this title on 30% PCW recycled paper. As a result, we have saved the
following resources: 31 trees, 22 million BTUs of energy, 3,2,764 lbs. of greenhouse gases,
11,472 gallons of water, and 1,473 lbs. of solid waste. For more information, please visit
our website, www.wisdompubs.org.

Contents

Eternal Peace

How to Use the Advice in This Book

This is a book of letters to people all over the world from Lama Zopa Rinpoche in response to requests for advice about their problems (all except four, which are letters Rinpoche wrote in response to various events).

Every word of advice Rinpoche gives is based on the teachings of the *Buddha*. In order to know how to use the advice in this book, therefore, it's necessary to understand the Buddha's views. In many cases, these views are radically different from those we commonly hold as unquestioned assumptions, both religious and materialist. In particular, it is useful to understand:

1. What is the mind?
2. Why good and bad things happen: karma
3. How to welcome the bad things: transforming problems into happiness
4. Compassion: working for others
5. Prayers and mantras

A Buddhist monk since his childhood in the mountains of Nepal, Rinpoche's expertise is the mind—the human heart and how to heal it. He is a master of the techniques that enable us to achieve what Buddha asserts is our innate potential for perfection, *enlightenment.*

- The development of the mind in this way is not a mystical process, a hit-and-miss affair,

which is often the way spiritual development is depicted. According to Buddha,

- It is a logical, rigorous, step-by-step procedure,
- Doable by everyone,
- That brings genuine, stable results: huge affection and empathy for others and the yearning to benefit them, and the unfailing ability to do so.

Rinpoche is the spiritual director of a worldwide network of Buddhist centers and activities devoted to helping others in this way, the Foundation for the Preservation of the *Mahayana* Tradition (FPMT).

Every word of advice Rinpoche gives is based on the teachings of the Buddha.

ix

He travels throughout the year, teaching at his centers and overseeing his projects, such as the building of the five-hundred-foot statue of *Maitreya*, the future Buddha, in northern India or the revitalizing of Mongolia's native Buddhist culture following its decay under decades of Communist rule. He also spends several months a year in meditation retreat.

Rinpoche receives more than three thousand letters a year at his office in Aptos, California, according to one of his secretaries, Australian nun Venerable Holly Ansett. A third of the letters are requests from the directors of his centers and projects; the rest are personal, from his students, requesting advice about their spiritual practice, their lives, their health, their families—and their problems.

"Rinpoche often doesn't start dictating until after midnight," Ven. Holly says. (Remarkably, Rinpoche does not seem to need sleep. When he is not traveling or teaching or dealing with his students and centers, he is meditating.) Rinpoche takes the folder of correspondence, which contains at least two hundred letters at any one time, and chooses the letters to reply to that evening. The letters that are urgent, such as those about the person's health, always go to the top of the pile.

Like many great masters, Rinpoche is skilled at recommending appropriate Tibetan herbal medicine. He often illustrates his letters with smiling faces or animals or sayings, or he may spend a long time writing out *mantras* in immaculate calligraphy, reproductions of some of which are included in these pages. Along with the appropriate practices and advice, Rinpoche often sends a book, blessed pills, a calendar, a Buddhist image, or other gift as well.

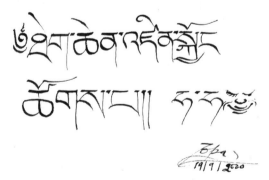

Rinpoche receives more than three thousand letters a year.

Foundation for the Preservation of the Mahayana Tradition. Ha! Ha!

Lama Zopa Rinpoche writing in gold one of hundreds of folios of The Sanghatasutra, *which will be put into the five-hundred-foot statue of Maitreya Buddha that he is building in northern India*

Letters rarely take less than two hours to answer, and sometimes they can be as long as thirty pages, written over several days. "We'll often leave the folder downstairs in the living room or in Rinpoche's room at night," says Ven. Holly. "Next day we'll find handwritten notes attached to letters, which I'll then transcribe."

Rinpoche is always moved by the kindness of others. "On flights, Rinpoche often remarks how kind the crew are," Ven. Holly says. "He thanks them, offers them gifts, writes out mantras for them and explains their meaning. In restaurants, he may offer the waitress a gift. They are always charmed by him!"

"When Rinpoche starts to answer a letter, it doesn't matter whether he has ever met the person, he will take their letter so seriously, never rushing it," says Ven. Holly. "He can spend hours deciding which

Rinpoche is always moved by the kindness of others.

practice is best, what advice to give, which flower postcard to send"—selected from hundreds of postcards that Rinpoche buys during his travels, mainly of flowers and nature, but also silly ones. "It is as if that person at that moment is the most special person in the world."

1. What Is the Mind?

For Buddha, the word "mind" refers to

> **The entire spectrum of our inner experiences: thoughts, feelings, tendencies, personality traits, perceptions, intuitions, and dreams.**

It functions in dependence upon the brain, but is itself

> **Not the brain, not physical.**

Not only that, our mind

> **Didn't come from our parents,**

> **Nor from a superior being.**

Our mind, or consciousness, is our own. It's not created by anybody else; it is its own entity. A river of mental moments, we can track it back and back to the first moment in our mother's womb, and back before that into countless past lives.

The job of a Buddhist is to delve into this mind of ours—"the workshop is in the mind," as Rinpoche puts it—and

> **Unravel the complex web of our innermost feelings by using Buddha's sophisticated psychological techniques, known as meditation.**

First we need to identify what's there, then understand it, and finally—this is the crux of the matter—change it. In fact, Buddha says,

> **We can change our mind to the point where we have rid it entirely of the neurotic emotions, the *delusions*, such as *attachment*, anger, self-hate, and jealousy, and**

> **Filled it full of the positive qualities, such as kindness, intelligence, and altruism.**

Our mind, or consciousness, is our own. It's not created by anybody else.

For most of us, the pursuit of this perfection, this *buddhahood*, does not come easily. But, as with the cultivation of any skill, we necessarily get better with practice. We all know that "practice makes perfect," or, as the

Tibetans would say, "nothing becomes more difficult with familiarity."

We usually give equal status to our neuroses and positive qualities and assume that the delusions are innate, that we're stuck with who we are. Buddha disagrees fundamentally. He says we can change, and this is because

- Our neuroses are like additives, pollution: they simply don't belong in the mind, and thus can be removed.

On the other hand,

- The positive qualities are at the core of our being; they define us; they are who we really are.

As we rid the mind of the delusions, the positive emotions naturally arise and grow. This is a natural, psychological process.

But merely believing this, Buddha says, won't help. We need to verify it for ourselves by engaging in the practices. What practice is, in fact, is the investigating of these assertions of the Buddha and making them our own experience, thus proving them to ourselves.

2. Why Good and Bad Things Happen: Karma

The power that propels the mind isn't outside it. Buddha calls this power *karma*. It occurs naturally. It wasn't revealed to him, nor did he make it up; like a scientist, he observed it to be so.

- Karma is the natural process of cause and effect occurring in the minds and lives of all living beings.

Every thought and feeling we have, along with what we do with our bodies and say with our speech as a result, is a karma, an "action," that necessarily brings a reaction in the future. Just naturally, like seeds,

- All positive actions ripen later as happiness (pleasing feelings and experiences), and
- All negative actions ripen as suffering (painful feelings and experiences).

Karma is a natural law. There is no other person involved in this process, punishing and rewarding us; there is no such concept in Buddhism.

Contrary to our deeply held assumption that people and events outside us are the main source of our experiences, that whatever happens to us is someone else's doing—God created us, our friends

Karma is a natural law. There is no other person involved in this process.

create our happiness, our enemies create our suffering—Buddha is saying, in effect, that

> ☙ **We are the creators of our own experiences, our own very selves.**

Our mind comes into this life fully programmed by our past actions, which, like seeds, ripen as our tendencies and experiences. We are propelled by the force of our own past karma, from moment to moment, from life to life.

> ☙ **From moment to moment, we create ourselves.**

A common mistake is to think that karma relates only to the bad things and to use it as a big stick to beat ourselves with. But all the good things—our human life itself, our health, our friends, our ability to get a job, our good qualities—are the result of our past actions as well.

> ☙ **There is nothing we experience, good or bad, that isn't the result of our own past actions.**

We'd be amazed and delighted if we realized just how hard we must have worked in past lives simply to be who we are now.

All of Rinpoche's advice is based on these assumptions about karma.

> ☙ **So, how do I apply karma, cause and effect, in my life?**

By remembering that my suffering and happiness are the result of my own past actions, I become empowered:

> ☙ **If I'm the main cause of who I am, then it follows I'm the main cause of what I can become. My life is in my own hands.**
>
> ☙ **It's up to me. I'm the boss.**

We'd be amazed and delighted if we realized just how hard we must have worked in past lives simply to be who we are now.

Given that I don't want suffering and do want happiness in the future, it follows that I must sow the seeds now: I need to abide by the law of karma:

> ☙ **Don't harm others,**
>
> ☙ **Try to help them, and**
>
> ☙ **Remove the delusions from my mind.**

This is the practice of the Buddha.

3. How to Welcome the Bad Things: Transforming Problems into Happiness

Rinpoche's advice is also based on the advanced practice called "transforming problems into happiness."

Suffering happens to all of us. It seems to come without warning, no matter how hard we try to avoid it. We assume it is bad, that it's not fair, and do everything we can to push it away, and when we can't we suffer even more.

What we need to do is interpret suffering in a different way.

> ● First, by understanding that everything we experience is the fruit of our past actions, that we are the creators of our own reality, we can greet the problem without panic, without self-pity or blame.

If we can change it, we do so; if not, we accept it. Just this changes our experience of it, lessens the suffering, calms the mind, and gives courage.

Not only that.

> ● Second, we can even feel good about the problem, be glad it's there.

As Rinpoche says, "The thought of liking problems should arise naturally, like the thought of liking ice cream!" We realize that the mere experiencing of the problem finishes the karma we created in the past that caused it; when a fruit ripens, the seed is finished.

> ● Third, if we welcome our problem as a challenge, we can actually use it to our advantage. Having problems then becomes a method for developing our amazing potential.

When it comes to achieving our ordinary life goals, we are full of admiration for the athletes, the businesspeople, and the artists who never give up in the face of incredible obstacles. We understand that their courage and perseverance in conquering the obstacles is what actually helps them accomplish their goals; it's a method in itself.

But when it comes to emotional problems, we don't have such courage. The moment the problem comes—the unkind word, the illness, the abuse—we feel victimized, angry, anxious, depressed.

> ● It seems almost perverse to think that these problems could be good.

"The thought of liking problems should arise naturally, like the thought of liking ice cream!"

- But with karma in mind and never losing sight of the goal, it's an approach that develops our own qualities and hugely opens our hearts to others.
- This approach is at the heart of the practice of the Buddhists of Tibet for the past thousand years.

The view of karma and responsibility for their own experiences is deep in their hearts; it's natural to them. It's exactly why His Holiness the Dalai Lama and his people have been able to deal so well with their suffering at the hands of the Chinese Communists since 1950.

- They are not angry at their oppressors,
- They don't wage war,
- They even have compassion for them.

When we're clear about our goal—the fulfillment of our own marvelous potential and the capacity to benefit others—welcoming our problems and transforming them into happiness is without doubt the quickest path to success.

- It's the most difficult practice, the most radical, but the most rewarding.

4. Compassion: Working for Others

Practicing in this way, it's inevitable that we open our hearts to others.

- We realize that we're all in the same boat: everyone is experiencing the fruits of their past actions and creating the causes for their future experiences.

And this includes the people who harm us.

- Many of the letters in this book are about the suffering that people experience at the hands of others.

Welcoming our problems and transforming them into happiness is without doubt the quickest path to success.

It's almost shocking to think that we can have compassion in response to this harm, but that is what Rinpoche repeatedly advises. As we are suffering now because of our own past actions, so too will they suffer in the future as a result of their present actions. How could we not have compassion?

- Like a mother for her destructive child, we can see that they are harming themselves.

5. Prayers and Mantras

Countless minds have achieved the perfection of enlightenment as Buddha describes it. Just naturally, these minds pervade the universe. How could it be any other way? When mind, which is not physical, is finally unencumbered by the delusions, how can it be confined by space or time or matter? It's not possible.

- These enlightened minds, which manifest in countless forms, constantly work for the sake of others.

Invoking these buddhas, reciting their mantras, and making prayers and requests to them are main methods for success in fulfilling our wishes, developing our qualities, and overcoming our problems.

- These practices give a rocket boost to our day-to-day job of developing our own minds, of becoming our own buddhas.

Tibetan Buddhism has a vast tradition of practices relating to the buddhas, which can be traced back to India and the time of *Shakyamuni Buddha* himself.

- Rinpoche recommends many of these practices to his students.

Does the Advice Apply to Me?

Read superficially, some of the instructions in the letters here may seem contradictory. But just as a medicine may be life-saving for one person and not helpful for another, Rinpoche customizes his advice depending on who is requesting it.

To find out whether it is relevant to us, as with all the advice of the Buddha, we should

- Read it carefully,
- Think about it, and
- If it seems appropriate, apply it in our lives.

Keep in Mind

- As students of Rinpoche, most letter writers actually used more honorific ways of addressing him than "Dear

Prayers and mantras give a rocket boost to our day-to-day job of developing our own minds.

Lama Zopa." Also, their names and locations have been changed and the letters themselves summarized.

- There are two lists at the end of this book: a *Glossary* of various Buddhist terms and *Mantras and Practices*, brief explanations of all the practices mentioned by Rinpoche, as well as many of the actual mantras. All terms and practices have been italicized in the text wherever they first occur.
- The full prayers, practices, and mantras can be found online at fpmt.org/DLZ.
- Teachings of Rinpoche, Lama Yeshe, and other lamas can be found at lamayeshe.com.

In *Dear Lama Zopa,* you hold in your hands a precious manual that shows us how to bravely go beyond the limits of our fearful sense of self and expand our hearts to encompass others.

Robina Courtin
San Francisco, March 2007

Acknowledgments

Many thanks for their editorial input to Norma Quesada, John Wolf, Diane Gregorio, David Kittelstrom, Gustavo Szpilman Cutz, Ven. Mindrol, and Amy Kittelstrom; for their paintings, to Peter Iseli (p. 71) and Jane Seidlitz (pp. 2, 183); and, for their photographs, to Ven. Roger Kunsang (pp. xi, 21, 164), and Ward Holmes (p. 53). The painting of Green Tara on page 147 is by the author. The words on the illustrations of animals on pages 17, 124, 127, 149, and 188 are by the author; the animals were painted by Dale Wright and Jonathan Partridge for a poster Rinpoche designed for Mary Alice Baldwin, to celebrate her kindness in offering land in California for a retreat center, thus protecting the animals that live there from being hunted.

You can read about the early years of Lama Zopa Rinpoche's life, and about his previous life as a meditator in the mountains of Solo Khumbu in Nepal, in Jamyang Wangmo's The Lawudo Lama *(Wisdom, 2005).*

The Letters

Shakyamuni Buddha

I Want to Stop Smoking

Dear Lama Zopa,
I need to stop smoking. How can I find the strength? I have tried so
many times. I have cut down, but I find it so hard, I just don't know
what to do. My partner smokes and sometimes it's such a nice social
time together when we go out for a cigarette, but I know it's bad for us
physically and mentally. It's an old habit and so much of my life goes
along with my cigarette breaks. Do you have any advice on how I can
quit once and for all?

Best wishes,
Denise, London

Dear Denise,
I am happy that you have cut down your smoking, as it is very harmful
to your body and life. It can shorten your life and cause cancer. It is said
both in Buddhist teachings and in ordinary life that smoking is harmful
and extremely distasteful.

> ◦ **The teachings say that the material used in cigarettes**
> **is impure, and that evil beings caused the substances**
> **to grow in order to interfere with people's practice**
> **of virtue, degenerate their minds, and engage them**
> **in nonvirtue, so that their minds are not free from**
> ***delusion.***

I once saw the body of a woman who died of lung cancer from
smoking, and her lungs were black and blue. A Tibetan doctor from
Dharamsala showed me one of her lungs. You could die like this if you
don't stop!

> ◦ **Smoking also makes people who don't smoke unhappy.**

Smoking pollutes your whole body, making it impure. It harms
your *subtle body*, too. It makes it difficult for virtuous thoughts to
arise, and it makes it very hard not to have attachment. Smoking just
brings temporary pleasure, and that's all. When you die, you don't take
one single benefit from smoking with you. It doesn't protect you from
suffering, and it can't help you achieve a good *rebirth* in your next life.

> ◦ **Think: "I am trying to become a champion, to defeat my**
> **delusions, especially my attachment. To do that I have**
> **to be strong."**

Smoking pollutes
your whole body,
making it impure.
It makes it very
hard not to have
attachment.

Some people spend their whole lives training for the Olympics. When they don't succeed, they experience unbelievable suffering because their attachment was so intense. You are trying to become a champion, to defeat your delusions, especially your attachment. If you can succeed against the enemy of delusions by avoiding smoking cigarettes, that would be fantastic.

Not following delusion also causes you to achieve *liberation* and helps you to reach enlightenment. Each time you avoid smoking you create the cause of realizations on the path to enlightenment. By defeating delusion, especially attachment, you will be able to liberate numberless *sentient beings* from eons of suffering in *samsara* and bring them to enlightenment.

> What better Olympic sport is there than this one? What better champion is there?

This way you become the most famous person among all sentient beings, not just in one country or in one world, but among all sentient beings— you become a buddha. Every day you have to have courage. Be brave.

> Also, you don't have to do everything that your boyfriend does. Your mind is not his. You are responsible for your own happiness.

With much love and prayers,

You are trying to become a champion, to defeat your delusions, especially your attachment. If you can succeed against the enemy of delusions by avoiding smoking cigarettes, that would be fantastic.

REMEMBER

- Smoking makes it hard for me to have virtuous thoughts.
- Every time I avoid smoking I create the cause for realizations on the path to enlightenment.
- I am responsible for my own happiness.

The Virus Was Undetectable

Dear Lama Zopa,

In 2003, I was admitted to hospital with AIDS-related pneumonia and vomiting. I had contracted HIV as a seventeen-year-old heroin user, but the virus had lain dormant until 1996, when I began to have bouts of pneumonia. I was treated with multiple-drug therapy, taking twenty tablets a day, but my condition deteriorated to the point where I had a T-cell count of zero.

I wrote to you from the hospital requesting your advice as to what practices I should perform. You wrote me a letter including specific practices, and I took your advice.

Six months later, when I went to my doctor for a checkup, the HIV virus was undetectable, and my T-cell count was 300. My doctor said that I no longer needed to take any medicine. I am writing to you to inform you of my recovery and to express my utmost thanks for saving my life.

> *My utmost gratitude, thanks, and devotion,*
> *Jane, Sydney*

My very dear Jane,

Thank you very much for your kind letter and gifts. I am extremely happy to hear of your recovery. That is so good, because human life is very precious and you only achieved this human rebirth through pure moral conduct in the past.

Now you have a precious human life, which is more valuable than a wish-fulfilling jewel. Having a precious human rebirth qualified with the *eight freedoms and ten richnesses,* allowing you to practice *Dharma* whenever you wish, is like a dream, a miracle.

You can practice:

1. The *Lesser Vehicle* path to achieve everlasting happiness and freedom from samsara.

2. The *Paramitayana* path of the *bodhisattva* to achieve full enlightenment, liberate numberless sentient beings from the oceans of samsaric sufferings, and bring them to enlightenment.

3. The *Tantra Vehicle* path to enable you to help others to achieve enlightenment more quickly.

I am extremely happy to hear of your recovery. That is so good, because human life is very precious and you only achieved this human rebirth through pure moral conduct in the past.

These are the most important reasons for having a long life and precious human rebirth.

Now, every day, you can plant the seed of the whole path to enlightenment. A long life gives you the opportunity to actualize the path, or at least to leave imprints on your mind of the whole path. This will create the causes for you to become enlightened so that you can benefit others and bring them to enlightenment.

Now you can spend the rest of your life practicing *Dharma*.

Please write any time.

With much love and prayers,

····· *One year later, Jane remains healthy.*

REMEMBER

- **I must use my precious human life to benefit others and become enlightened.**

Which Practices Should I Do?

Dear Lama Zopa,

I have just learned that I have an AIDS-related illness and I am feeling very scared. I don't want to die, and I can't believe this has happened to me. I realize that we will all die at some point, but you just don't think about it for yourself until something like this happens.

My practice has not been good lately, Rinpoche. But now with this sickness, I feel I must go back to it. I'm happy to do whatever practices you recommend. I have heard of people with AIDS being cured by practice and by Tibetan medicine. I don't want to have any false hopes, but do you think there is a chance I could get better?

I try to have the attitude of transforming problems, but it's very difficult.

Many prayers of gratitude,
Javier, Texas

Now, every day, you can plant the seed of the whole path to enlightenment.

My dear Javier,

Thank you for your letter.

According to my divinations, it would be good for you

1. **To take** *inner-offering pills,* **nine a day for five months. You can get these from a Tibetan medical center.**

2. **To take Western medicine.**

3. **To perform** *prostrations* **to the** *Thirty-five Buddhas.* **If you can't actually prostrate, put your palms together and visualize making prostrations to the** *Guru Puja merit field,* **which includes the Thirty-five Buddhas. Recite the buddhas' names, with a clear visualization and strong purification.**

4. **To look at your HIV status as a positive thing, not a negative one.**

You are actually extremely fortunate because you can generate *bodhichitta* for all sentient beings, especially those who have AIDS-related illnesses. So, please use it to generate strong bodhichitta.

 ➤ **Think: "I can purify past negative** *karma,* **accumulate extensive** *merit,* **and so achieve enlightenment quickest."**

According to my experience, particularly with AIDS,

 ➤ **it is** *very* **important to keep the mind happy as much as possible, and strong.**

That makes one's life longer. The sickness won't manifest as much and can also decrease, depending on your practice and on how powerful your positive thinking is, for instance, your compassion for others.

 ➤ **You can think of all the suffering beings who have AIDS.**

For example, there was one student who was HIV-positive. He received instructions from his *guru* in Dharamsala, a very high lama, who gave him some advice about performing the bodhichitta practice "exchanging oneself for others"—*tonglen*—which means taking on other sentient beings' sufferings and giving one's happiness and merit to others. The student did this practice for four days. Then he went to the hospital and they could not find the HIV virus. This was the same hospital that had diagnosed him. I asked him how long he had practiced each time. He said he had practiced for only a few minutes. Even though the duration was so short, his compassion was incredibly strong. Every time he did this meditation, he cried a lot.

One student who was HIV-positive received instructions from his guru in Dharamsala about performing bodhichitta practice—taking on other sentient beings' sufferings and giving one's happiness and merit to others. The student did this practice for four days. Then he went to the hospital and they could not find the HIV virus.

- Just thinking about others' suffering made him weep. Because his compassion for others was so strong, it purified so much of his negative karma, including the cause for manifesting his condition.

So, this example shows the incredible effect that some meditational experiences have on healing. It is a sign of purification. It also keeps your spirits high and makes life peaceful and happy.

There is a difference between being concerned about your own suffering and being concerned for others' suffering, having compassion. The effect is different.

- With concern for your own problems, there is attachment and worries about attachment and about *ego*. The effect is not peaceful.

- But concern and compassion for others, even though it's a kind of worry, has a peaceful effect. Its effect on one's own mental continuum is positive.

Love and prayers,

REMEMBER

- My HIV status is a positive thing, not a negative one.
- I must keep my mind happy.
- Concern and compassion for others makes me peaceful.
- Compassion can heal.

An Inconvenient Truth

..... *Rinpoche wrote to the American politician Al Gore after seeing his film,* An Inconvenient Truth, *in September 2006.*

My Very Dear Honorable Al Gore,
I heard about your very inspiring movie, *An Inconvenient Truth*. I and a number of monks and nuns *(sangha),* all from different countries, as well as other Buddhists, went to see it. It is quite shocking to see the truth: what is happening in the world, where the world is going, particularly what is happening in the U.S.A. It's quite amazing…and all based on money, just to produce more money.

Already the problems have started happening: so many people are experiencing the danger of global warming, the danger of floods, melting snow and ice. All this will soon endanger many more people around the world, including in the U.S.A. Even in the Tibetan capital, Lhasa, it has become warmer. It wasn't like this before; there has been a change.

> **My conclusion is that it's all because of people's lack of education on these issues, people's lack of awareness that what they do in the world has an effect; people are not being mindful; they do not understand this.**

I and all the monks and nuns and Buddhist students who went to see your movie highly appreciate your efforts to reveal the truth, exposing and introducing the truth to the world.

> **Please continue taking responsibility to benefit this world, to reduce suffering, and to bring peace and happiness to this world.**

The ultimate thing is for people to develop a good heart, for everyone to live happily, only benefiting each other, including between the different religions, and including animals (there are so many when compared to humans).

With prayers for your long life, for your wishes to benefit others to succeed, and, if you can, especially to help His Holiness the Dalai Lama and the Tibetan people have total political and religious freedom, like before; for the people to be guided by His Holiness the Dalai Lama. This is what the majority of Tibetans are anxiously, very earnestly, wanting.

Sincerely yours,
Lama Zopa Rinpoche

I and all the monks and nuns and Buddhist students who went to see your movie highly appreciate your efforts to reveal the truth, exposing and introducing the truth to the world.

Fed Up with Anger

Dear Lama Zopa,

Recently, when I became angry, I was thinking during my morning prayers about how happy I would be if I were never angry again. I reflected how there had never been a reason for being angry, and yet the moments of anger kept returning. Feeling very sad about this, I prayed to Lama Yeshe and to you for help.

Then the phone rang as I was starting my morning in the office, and it was you wanting to talk with me.

Your first question was, "How was your night?" and I replied that I had had a bad night. I told you that I'd been thinking about my anger and wanted to get rid of it. This seemed to please you, and you gave me such wonderful advice.

I just wanted to write to thank you so much for your continued advice and support.

> *Best wishes,*
> *Bernadette, Dublin*

····· *The response below is a written version of the advice Rinpoche gave to Bernadette over the telephone.*

Bernadette,

It's very good if you feel some *aversion* to your anger. It helps you to free yourself from samsara. If you develop aversion toward anger and all the delusions, it helps you to reach enlightenment quickly. Without aversion toward delusions, nothing happens.

In the West, the way of thinking is the opposite of this. They think you need to have desire, anger, and a strong ego. They think it's not possible to live without a strong ego, so they build it up.

> ◆ Think: "By following delusions, I only create negative karma. I am looking for happiness, but by following desire, anger, and other delusions, I will only experience suffering."

Following our delusions leads to rebirths in *lower realms*, as *hell* beings, *hungry ghosts*, or animals. Even as a human being, you experience much suffering, and you create negative karma again and again by following anger, desire, and all the delusions.

If you develop aversion toward anger and all the delusions, it helps you to reach enlightenment quickly. Without aversion toward delusions, nothing happens.

That is why

🍂 **It is good to develop aversion to your anger.**

By having aversion toward anger, desire, attachment—all the delusions—you start to give up these delusions. You realize their harmfulness. Aversion toward delusions is the only way to be free from them. It's a good sign. It means you are getting closer to enlightenment, and to becoming beneficial for all sentient beings.

REMEMBER

- It is good to develop aversion to my delusions; it's the only way to get rid of them.
- I want to be happy so I must give up anger and the other delusions.

ANGER

My Anger Harms People

Dear Lama Zopa,

I am one of the art editors in a small advertising agency, and I supervise a number of people in my division. When people do not meet the deadlines, or turn in sloppy work, or waste time at the office, etc., I really lose my temper. As a result, I have hurt quite a few people with my angry outbursts and have lost some valuable employees who have walked out on the job. They just couldn't deal with me anymore.

Is it possible to correct inappropriate behavior on the part of my staff without becoming angry? Or is this an occasion when my anger is beneficial and I should just accept that some people won't like it and may leave? In what ways might my anger be harming myself and others? I would welcome so much any advice you could give me on this matter.

Best wishes,
Christian, Oslo

You are looking for happiness, but by following desire, anger, and other delusions, you will only experience suffering.

11

My very dear Christian,

This is really an opportunity to practice the path of patience. The purpose of practicing patience is to have immediate peace and happiness within you.

> ✒ Think: "That moment when I don't get angry means I don't harm myself, I don't cause myself unhappiness."

When the mind becomes negative, it is like a bomb inside you. If you are killed in a war by an external bomb, it doesn't necessarily mean you have to be born in the lower realms—you may be born in the *upper realms*. The bomb of anger, however, is billions of times worse for you than any external bomb. When it arises, you create negative karma and throw yourself into the three lower realms, where you have to experience terrible suffering for an incredibly long time—for eons!

In *A Guide to the Bodhisattva's Way of Life,* Shantideva says that the negative karma created by one second of anger causes us to experience the three lower realms for eons—we can't be reborn in the realm of a happy *transmigratory being*. This is without even mentioning the negative karma collected from our angry actions in infinite past lives.

He also says that the merit collected for one thousand years by making charity and offerings to those gone to bliss and so forth is destroyed by one second of anger.

Each time you stop being angry by practicing patience, this becomes your most practical contribution to world peace.

So, there are several disadvantages to anger.

1. **The first disadvantage is how much anger causes you to suffer in the three lower realms.**

2. **The second is how anger destroys eons of merit.**

3. **The third disadvantage is that anger delays realizations, depending on whom you get angry with and whom you create the negative karma with.**

4. **The fourth is that anger also causes you to have an ugly body in your future lives. Practicing patience brings you a beautiful body in future lives.**

In this way, getting angry is unbelievably harmful to yourself. Being angry just one time is so harmful, so you can imagine if it happens all day long or for weeks, months, or years. It is terrifying to think about. Just being angry one time brings so much suffering.

➤ **Think: "If I am angry I can't really work with others."**

They get upset and leave, because they are so unhappy with you, and seeing this also makes you unhappy. Also, if you get angry, it makes others angry, and then this makes you angry again! You make yourself the target for others to get angry at you and harm you with harsh speech and dislike. If anger gets worse, it can even cause physical harm.

If you are patient, you don't get angry at sentient beings. In that way, sentient beings only receive peace and happiness from you.

➤ **Each time you stop being angry by practicing patience, this becomes your most practical contribution to world peace. It brings so much peace and happiness to your own world, mind, and heart.**

➤ **For others, it brings peace and happiness, not only for beings in this world, but for all living beings.**

➤ **If you are able to practice patience in this life, it will be much easier in future lives.**

At your work, you can change the staff if you don't like them, but that will happen over and over, and it is difficult to bring your mind to peace. Whereas with patience, your mind is happy all the time. Your evaluations at work may be correct, but the problem is the way they are expressed—with harsh words and anger. These are extra and unnecessary; they create the problems. Of course, someone doing wrong needs to have it explained to them, but this should be delivered with compassion for them and with no negative feelings.

With patience, your mind is happy all the time.

13

A

➤ **You should use only kind words, even though you are saying what they did is wrong. And along with compassion you need *wisdom*.**

You have a great opportunity to gain experience in patience. Each time you wake up, you must plan this—especially today! If you don't make a firm plan in the morning, you won't remember the teachings when anger comes up.

The more you cherish others in daily life, the less anger you will have. Think that each person you meet is the source of so much past happiness and will be the source of so much future happiness, including the realizations of the path to enlightenment. So, respect others and practice kindness toward them, especially toward those who get angry with you.

So, to conclude:

1. **Practice patience,**

2. **Cherish others by remembering their kindness,**

3. **Respect others, and**

4. **Practice kindness to others.**

Then, everyone will love and support you and be your friend. They will be surprised and change their minds about you. They will be inspired when they see that your mind can change and develop.

Thank you very much.

With much love and prayers,

Respect others and practice kindness toward them, especially toward those who get angry with you.

REMEMBER

- **The bomb of anger is worse than any external bomb.**
- **My anger makes others dislike me.**
- **Patience makes me peaceful.**
- **The more I cherish others, the less angry I'll be.**

The Crocodile Hunter

Rinpoche wrote to Terri Irwin, the widow of Steve Irwin, the Crocodile Hunter, after he was killed by a stingray in September 2006.

My very dear Terri,

I am sending you my condolences for our dear Steve Irwin, who is known to the world as the Crocodile Hunter—maybe even known to the snakes and crocodiles as well.

I watched Steve Irwin so many times on television, for so many years: Steve catching snakes and crocodiles, letting them go, and also helping them, and all his incredible excitement. It made me curious when I was watching him, his being very active, how his life would end, whether one day he would be killed by one of those animals.

When I heard the news I immediately did prayers, chanting many mantras and prayers for him, purifying anything that causes suffering. I made prayers for the best thing to happen to him.

You and your family must be very sad, but since you have a strong bond with him, according to Buddhist philosophy you have created the cause to meet him again.

> **He may not *reincarnate* in the same shape or body, but, like the flame of a candle, when you light another one from it, the flame continues.**

Please continue your good heart, bringing peace to the world, to human beings—and to the animals, who are the largest number in the world when compared with humans. Continue to give your love to them.

Thank you very much.

With much love and prayers,
Lama Zopa Rinpoche

Please continue your good heart, bringing peace to the world, to human beings—and to the animals, who are the largest number in the world when compared with humans. Continue to give your love to them.

Animal Liberation

Dear Rinpoche,
I feel very sad when I think about all the creatures that are killed. Even if everybody were vegetarian, so many animals would still get killed. Are there some practices I can do to help at least some of them?
Much love,
Mary, Melbourne

Dear Mary,
One of the things you can do for animals and insects is to save them from being killed. I started a particular tradition of liberating animals in which we set animals and insects free in a safe environment. At our house, we have three or four animal-liberation practices every month. We buy worms and insects (you can also buy lobsters or fish or even bigger animals) who would otherwise be killed.

But not only do we simply save their lives. We carry them around a *stupa* as many times as possible. We chant mantras and blow on water, which we then sprinkle on them, and then we liberate them into water or the earth, according to the kinds of creatures they are. Not only does this liberate them from the lower realms, but it also creates the cause for their enlightenment.

If you don't have a stupa you can

1. **Put many holy objects, such as buddha images and texts, on a table in the middle of a room.**

2. **While carrying the insects or animals, walk around the table as many times as you like, reciting mantras or other prayers.**

If you have many ants in your house, you might kill them out of carelessness. If instead you are careful, you can

1. **Pick them up with a soft tissue paper, cotton, a broom, or a feather, and put them in a plastic bag with some food in it that they like, and then close the bag.**

2. **Take it around the holy objects as many times as you can.**

3. **Then put them outside, releasing them by opening the plastic bag, or by shaking it on the ground with the food.**

I started a particular tradition of liberating animals in which we set animals and insects free in a safe environment. We buy worms and insects (you can also buy lobsters or fish or even bigger animals) who would otherwise be killed.

We have many insects, so every day

1. **We catch as many as possible in large jars that have ventilation and space.**

2. **We separate the various kinds of insects into different jars so they do not fight or frighten each other.**

3. **We *circumambulate* them around our large altar that is full of holy objects, running as fast as possible so that we perform as many circumambulations as we can, with the jars full of insects.**

4. **Then we release them outside.**

The only way you can help ants and other insects is if they come into your house. This is a very good way, an excellent opportunity, to benefit them, in addition to offering them charity by giving them food. Taking them around the holy objects is the charity of offering them Dharma; saving their lives is the *charity of fearlessness*. By purifying their minds, you're saving them from suffering.

> ☙ **If there are 1,000 statues and holy objects on the table or altar, then if you circumambulate the animals once, it creates 1,000 causes to achieve enlightenment, liberation from samsara, a good rebirth, and happiness in future lives.**

Each time you carry or lead the animals around the table it creates that many causes for their happiness and long lives. So, if you carry a billion insects around holy objects, you are offering enlightenment to that many sentient beings each time you circumambulate. This is really fantastic, the most amazing benefit that you can offer to other beings.

There is a story about an eighty-year-old man. He entered the Mahayana path, and when the time ripened, he became enlightened and performed perfect works for sentient beings, bringing them to enlightenment. All that perfect work—enlightening all those beings—came from his being enlightened, which was in turn a result of having entered the Mahayana path. Before that he was an *arhat* and actualized the path to liberation, which was itself a result of being a monk. He had been able to become a monk because, eons ago, he was a fly following some cow dung flowing in a rivulet around a stupa, an act that became a circumambulation of the stupa. All these benefits—being an arhat, being enlightened, and enlightening sentient beings—depended on the small merit of following the smell of cow dung around a stupa.

> ❧ We should always keep in mind how precious even one circumambulation is, how precious it is to take animals around holy objects. When human beings circumambulate intentionally it has incredible benefit.

According to the law of karma, even small actions, both positive and negative, can ripen in huge results. Since karma is expandable, we shouldn't be careless, even with a small amount of merit. Each holy object is so powerful and can liberate so many beings from suffering and bring them to enlightenment, causing us to actualize the path.

> ❧ Also, it is extremely good to save beings from being killed to be eaten as food.

Lobsters are boiled alive in hot water. We can only imagine how immense the suffering would be. If it were us, we would try every single way to get out, but they are trapped, and not only that, they can't communicate with us.

Like us, all beings want happiness and do not want suffering, problems, or discomfort.

With much love and prayers,

REMEMBER

- Like us, all beings want happiness and do not want suffering, problems, or discomfort.
- Taking animals around holy objects creates the cause for their future happiness and enlightenment.

Lobsters are boiled alive in hot water. If it were us, we would try every single way to get out, but they are trapped, and not only that, they can't communicate with us.

How to Help My Cat?

Dear Lama Zopa,
I have a cat. I've been thinking lately that her life must be one of suffering, just sitting there in her ignorance every day. How can she create any good karma? It doesn't seem possible. Can you tell me some things that I can do to help her mind?

Love,
James, Amsterdam

My dear James,

You're right. It's not enough that you look after animals and that they give you comfort. You must do something of practical benefit for them. This is what you can do every day:

1. **Circumambulate with her around holy objects, chanting mantras. [See page 16.]**

2. **You can recite prayers or mantras in her ears to plant the seed of all the realizations of the path to enlightenment. Or you can play CDs of prayers and mantras so that she can hear them.**

This makes a huge difference. It has incredible results, enabling her to have a good rebirth in her next life, to be born as a human being and meet the Dharma.

There is a story about when the Buddha gave teachings to five hundred swans in a field and in their next lives they were born as humans, became monks, and all became *arya* beings, highly realized beings who are able to achieve the cessation of suffering and the true path. The result from just hearing Dharma words was incredible.

Vasubandhu used to recite the *Abhidharmakosha,* and a pigeon on the roof heard this every day. One day the pigeon died and Vasubandhu used his clairvoyance to check to see where it had been reborn. It was born human to a family who lived in the valley below. He went down and visited the child and asked if he could look after him, and the family let the child go with him. The child became a monk named Lopon Loden and became an expert on the text that he had heard when he was a pigeon. He wrote four commentaries on that text.

3. **You can also give her a *Dharma name* rather than a useless name that has no benefit for her. Then, every time you call her name, it leaves a positive imprint on her mind.**

We call our dog Om Mani Padme Hum, the compassion mantra. Each time she hears her name it plants the seed for the whole path to enlightenment in her mind, leaving a positive imprint. It also creates the cause for her to understand all the 84,000 teachings of the Buddha because they are contained in the mantra *Om mani padme hum*: the *two truths,* the path of *method and wisdom,* and the goal: *dharmakaya* and *rupakaya.* Each time she hears her name it brings her closer to enlightenment. This is such an easy way to benefit animals.

4. **It's also extremely good to bless food before you give it to your cat. Recite the *Five Powerful Mantras for***

Vasubandhu used to recite the, Abhidharmakosha, and a pigeon on the roof heard this every day. In its next life, the pigeon became a monk named Lopon Loden and became an expert on the text that he had heard when he was a pigeon.

19

Liberating Sentient Beings from the Lower Realms or the mantras of the *Compassion Buddha, Medicine Buddha,* and *Milarepa,* and then blow on the food.

If you can't do it every time you feed her, then you can bless her entire supply of food at the same time.

> ● This has power and helps anyone who eats this food to not be reborn in the lower realms; it blesses their mind and purifies negative karma.

Much love and prayers,

REMEMBER

- Reciting prayers and mantras into my pet's ears leaves imprints in her mind that ripen in her future life, causing her to receive spiritual teachings.
- Blessing her food helps her purify negative karma.

My Aging Dog

Dear Rinpoche,

My dog is old now. When it comes time for her to die, I'd rather not have her put down, but I really want to help her. Please tell me some practices I can do that will help her mind then. And what can I do to help once she is dead?

Many thanks,
Roberta, Sydney

Dear Roberta,

What you can do for your dog when she is dying is keep her in a quiet place where she won't be disturbed. Then you can do either of the following:

1. Perform Medicine Buddha practice, visualizing the seven *Medicine Buddhas* on the crown of the animal, absorbing into the animal.

2. Perform the Thirty-five Buddhas practice, visualizing nectar coming into her through the crown of her head,

purifying her negative karma. Take strong *refuge* in the buddhas to protect and guide her.

And after she has died you can:

1. Recite the *Chenrezig* mantra and other mantras such as those of Milarepa and *Namgyelma* and then blow strongly over her body after each mantra.

2. Or, after reciting a mantra, you can blow on water, visualizing each of the buddhas absorbing into the water; each drop has the power to purify negative karmas.

3. Then you can pour the water on her body and think that all her negative karma is purified.

If practical, it would be good to leave her body undisturbed for a couple of days after she has died because her mind might not have left her body yet.

Much love and prayer,

REMEMBER

- Keep my dog in a quiet place when she is dying and if possible for a couple of days after she is dead.

We call our dog Om Mani Padme Hum, the compassion mantra.

How to Check Before Getting Pregnant

Dear Lama Zopa,
I would like to know what I can do to make sure that if I get pregnant there will not be any difficulties, such as the baby being deformed. Is that possible?

Love and many thanks,
Mary, Sydney

Dear Mary,

Because we are not *omniscient* or clairvoyant, we may want to consult a qualified astrologer for certain decisions. Before you decide to get pregnant, four things can be checked astrologically:

1. **Harmonious body—referring to you and your partner. If this is not harmonious then children may be born deformed or may not live long.**

2. **Harmonious authority—If this is good then you will have a lot of success in business.**

3. **Harmonious life—If this is not good you and your partner will only have a short life together.**

4. **Harmonious good luck—If this is positive you will have good fortune.**

It is important to check if these four things are harmonious or not. If they are not harmonious but you still want to have a child with your partner, there are astrological methods to help prevent negative outcomes, such as a child being ill or deformed.

In general, before beginning any significant endeavor, for your own safety and to prevent hardships, difficulties, or too much suffering, it is good to check these four things with an expert in either Tibetan or Chinese astrology.

With much love and prayers,

There are astrological methods to prevent negative outcomes, such as a child being ill or deformed.

22

How Can I Stop Attachment?

Dear Lama Zopa,
I have many attachments in my life that drain my energy more than they
should. I worry about the people close to me more than they need me to
worry about them. I often feel that I could be more effective as a person if
I could break free and focus on developing skills and abilities that really
matter. But I am totally caught up in worrying about my friends and
possessions. How can I make progress?

Love,
Jill, Amsterdam

Dear Jill,
Especially for us beginners, one of the most powerful ways to counteract
attachment is to think of *death and impermanence.*

> ✎ Think: "I can die any time. So, too, can the object of
> attachment, the other person, die at any time."

Death is one thing, but other changes can come about, too. The
object can change and become undesirable. Any day, any moment, this
can happen. An accident could happen, our body could get damaged
or become deformed. The body can change at any time. It can contract
leprosy. Many things like that can happen.

One very effective practice is:

> ✎ Think: "Any day, any minute, the object of my
> attachment can become my enemy by doing something
> that my attachment doesn't like."

No Desire
No Desire means
No Problems, inner
happiness satisfaction.
HA HA

The more imprints
of attachment
that are left on the
mind, the more
attachment will
arise strongly over
and over again,
causing many
difficulties in the
future.

The person can say or do something that your *self-cherishing* doesn't want. For example, the person may come to like another person and lose interest in you. This can happen at any time.

Also:

➤ **Think: "If I allow attachment to arise, it leaves a negative imprint on my mind, which makes attachment arise again and again."**

That makes it more difficult to handle attachment in the future. The more imprints that are left, the more attachment will arise strongly over and over again, causing many difficulties in the future. It's good to remember that this makes your life very uncontrolled.

With much love and prayers,

REMEMBER

- I could die at any moment.
- The object of my attachment can easily change into the object of my aversion.

Making Your Life Beneficial

Dear Lama Zopa,
I have a nice home and I love my husband very much. I think that generally I am happy. But sometimes I get depressed and worried that my life is going by and that I am not doing more to make it meaningful. I see that there is a lot of suffering in the world, but I don't know what I can do. I think perhaps I am too attached to the comfort and beauty of my home and to my husband, especially to the sexual relationship we have.

When the environment around me has no beauty or pleasure in it, I am not happy and even become angry! I do not want to live for myself alone, but I am also afraid of being without all these things that I like. I want to make my life more beneficial for others but I think maybe these strong feelings of attachment sometimes make it difficult for me to think of others. Please tell me how I can live a better life.

Best wishes,
Maria, Colombia

If you live your life only thinking about your own pleasure, from this comes only pain.

Dear Maria,

If you are performing the actions of your daily life with the two following attitudes, you are getting close to enlightenment:

1. **Meditation on the *lamrim*—the stages of the path to enlightenment—the teachings on impermanence, karma, *renunciation*, compassion, and so on.**

This can mean living your life with the wish to achieve enlightenment quickly or at least to prepare your mind by leaving positive imprints on it every day.

2. **Cultivating a sincere heart, doing social service with compassion: in other words, working for others.**

This means doing something for others, from your heart. Even if you can give only a little help, you still get real satisfaction, like you have done something meaningful and positive with your life. Then, every day, every moment, every second, you are getting closer to enlightenment.

If your life does not have these two things in them, then no matter how much you meditate, you are only doing it for yourself. Your life becomes dark, because everything is done with self-cherishing, desire, attachment, and clinging to this life. All of these are nonvirtues. When you die, you don't have any positive thoughts, and you are not able to renounce life.

You are looking for pleasure for yourself, with attachment, and from this comes only pain:

1. **There is the pain of separation, where you can't stand to be away from a person to whom you are attached. Then, each day, your feelings become stronger, until the attachment becomes unbearable.**

2. **Then there comes the pain of jealousy of others.**

3. **You have so many worries and fears, and it becomes so much suffering.**

You have so many projections, so many anxieties and fears. If something changes or happens to the person to whom you are attached, for example, he or she is no longer interested in you, or leaves you for someone else, then you feel incredible pain. It is as if a disaster or war has happened in your mind. You are attacked by your own hallucinations, fears, and so forth, and you harm yourself and the other person. Your life becomes a huge movie of violent negative karma. Then there is nothing to rejoice in and no virtue to dedicate. Your mind is very sad and dissatisfied.

There is a big difference between enjoying your life with the thought of benefiting others and enjoying things just for your own pleasure, just for yourself. Even sex done with a wish to benefit merely the person you are with becomes a cause for future happiness.

- With attachment your life is totally wasted. You don't achieve anything meaningful, and you die with regret, because your life had no purpose and then it was finished.

- When you die, you don't have any positive thoughts, and you are not able to renounce life.

- You die with all the negative karmas that you have collected every day in your life, every minute, every hour, every day, every year, because nothing has been purified.

- Not only that, but the negative karma has also grown, so you go to the lower realms.

You could have had a long life and happiness, the happiness of future lives, a peaceful mind in daily life, and your own ultimate happiness. You could have performed spiritual practice, meditation, purified negative karma, and collected merit. Instead you followed attachment. Most people in the world do not know about this. They have no idea, and their whole life is spent living in pure attachment, in sexual pleasure, and that's it.

All suffering comes from living with attachment. You can see how the world is suffering in this way. You can see how people who do not have any idea about this are suffering now and creating even more suffering for the future.

All suffering comes from living with attachment. You can see how the world is suffering in this way. You can see how people who do not have any idea about this are suffering now and creating even more suffering for the future.

If you don't apply the meditations, then even a small amount of attachment is so much suffering. When you think of people who are never involved in positive actions—offering service for others or having compassion—you can see how their entire life is suffering. Their life is wasted; even their future is wasted. If they spend their lives pursuing only this life's happiness, such as being a famous singer, actor, or president, their lives are totally wasted, without meaning.

- If you are not able to renounce life 100 percent, which means to renounce desire and clinging to this life, and

- If you are not able to do social service (working for others) or practice the path to enlightenment, then your life has no meaning. It is empty and wasted.

Not only that, it also becomes negative, and creates future sufferings, one after the other. You will have to experience them; they only come back to you.

❧ **How much peace and happiness you experience depends on your attitude.**

If you have attachment and your main goal is to obtain freedom for yourself alone, then you are creating negativity all the time, and you are not creating positive emotions like compassion and loving kindness. If your main goal is desire, attachment, and clinging to this life, and if other sentient beings are not important to you, then you are creating more negativity and a more unhappy life. However, if your Dharma practice is to benefit others, then you will have more peace and happiness, even if you have not completely renounced this life. If others are the most important thing in your life, then you will have happiness. If others come first in your heart, you will have so much peace and happiness and fewer emotional problems.

❧ **Your positive attainments and actions depend on how much you guard yourself from following negative thoughts and how much you keep a positive attitude.**

It all depends on how well you protect your mind from attachment and thoughts of self-cherishing. There is a big difference between enjoying your life with the thought of benefiting others and enjoying things just for your own pleasure, just for yourself. Even sex done with a wish to benefit merely the person you are with becomes a cause for future happiness.

These two attitudes—lamrim and the good heart—make an unbelievably huge difference in your life. With them, the sun is shining, without them, life is dark and obscured because of attachment and a negative attitude. It is like the difference between the sky and the earth.

Love and prayers,

REMEMBER

. . . .

- I will think about impermanence, karma, and the path to enlightenment every day.
. . . .
- I will live my life, even enjoying what pleasure it brings, with the wish to benefit others.
. . . .
- All my suffering comes from living with attachment.

If others are the most important thing in your life, then you will have happiness. If others come first in your heart, you will have so much peace and happiness, and you will have fewer emotional problems.

The Object of Attachment Is a Hallucination

Dear Lama Zopa,

I am really struggling with so much attachment and desire for my girlfriend. It comes out the most in my jealousy toward other people she spends time with, even her family and friends. This jealousy is making me do things I wouldn't normally do, like getting angry and yelling at her for small things. I end up fighting with her so much that it feels like we are more enemies than friends. I feel ashamed of how I am acting, and I'm afraid she'll eventually leave me if I don't stop this behavior, but I feel stuck and don't know how to get out of this pattern.

Best wishes,
Derek, Norwich

Dear Derek,

    ☞ **Strengthen your mind and motivate yourself.**

    ☞ **Attachment obscures the mind and prevents it from realizing *emptiness*.**

It leads you to create negative karma, such as the *ten nonvirtuous actions*, and causes you to break the *three vows*: the *pratimoksha vows*, which are the foundation, the ground, the earth from where liberation comes; the *bodhisattva vows*; and the *tantric vows*, which enable you to achieve enlightenment quickly.

    ☞ **Attachment cannot cut the root of samsara, and one will abide and suffer endlessly in samsara.**

Therefore, we must win over our delusions and defeat the enemy—attachment. Attachment has kept us in samsara from time without beginning, causing us to suffer in the *six realms*.

    ☞ **Attachment is like honey on a razor, appearing helpful on the surface but in fact destroying and cheating us.**

We may believe a self-existent beautiful woman is standing there, but actually she is not; our mind is making it up. Due to our own hallucination, we believe in the appearance, but it is like a dream or a movie. We project a real woman, but it is not as it appears. We are attached to that hallucination 100 percent, believing there is something real there that we can have, but it doesn't exist. It's a projection of our ignorant mind, which believes in the *inherently existent* woman.

> *We may believe there is a beautiful woman standing there, but actually she is not there; it's our own mind. Due to our own hallucination it is like a dream or a movie. We project a real woman, but it is not as it appears.*

- Always keep in mind: One who smiles at you, who praises you, and who shows affection to you, bolsters your ego; in this sense, your real enemy is that person.

You can still stay with your companion and not get angry at her. Just keep some perspective and distance mentally, as a part of your renunciation, for this stops you from being attached.

Love and prayers,

REMEMBER

- I must win over my delusions and defeat the enemy, attachment.
- I must stop believing in my own projections.

Attachment has kept us in samsara from time without beginning, causing us to suffer in the six realms.

Should I Have a Baby?

Dear Lama Zopa,

I am writing to ask your advice on a personal decision I am having trouble making. I have always thought I would have a baby someday, and I am approaching the age where I have to decide one way or the other.

I feel confused because, on the one hand, raising a child as a Buddhist may be a good contribution to the world. On the other hand, I worry that I am not advanced enough in my spiritual practice to be a good role model for a child and may do a horrible job.

What would be the best for me to do, Rinpoche? What's the best way to think?

With love,
Svetlana, St. Petersburg

My dear Svetlana,

A mother has to bear great hardships for her child and sacrifice many things. She experiences a lot of pain during childbirth and then looks after her child day and night. She is always cleaning up poop and pee-pee and doesn't get to rest. She bears so many burdens. As the child grows up, there are also many problems for the parents. They have to provide food, clothing, and education.

> ✹ **If children recognize their parents' loving sacrifices and take these inspiring beings as role models, then all the parents' work will have been worthwhile.**

I advise people to plan carefully before having a child. If the parents can look ahead and do this, then the child is able to bring benefit to the world.

With much love and prayers,

I advise people to plan carefully before having a child. If the parents can look ahead and do this, then the child is able to bring benefit to the world.

REMEMBER

- A mother has to bear great hardships to bring up a child properly.
- Parents who gladly makes sacrifices for their children's benefit can be inspiring role models.

Buddha Baby

Dear Lama Zopa,

My partner and I are so very happy with our new baby. We wanted to let you know about him so that he might be in your prayers. We love our baby so much, and we want all that is good for him throughout his life, but the thought of him living in this world causes me some anxiety. What will he have to face? How will my partner and I influence his development? I can pray for his good fortune, but how can I benefit him in our practical, day-to-day interactions? Even the best intentions do not always seem to bring about good results.

What can we do for our child to further his development as a good human being?

Love,
Edie, Colorado

My very dear Edie,
How are you? I am sure you are in bliss all the time, ecstatic. I hope you, your partner, and the baby are well. I hope you are having a great time with your Buddha baby. How is he doing?

> ❧ **I am sure you are learning a lot from him, all the time, every day—**

learning about life; the mind; samsara and the nature of samsara; the importance of liberation, nirvana, and enlightenment; about compassion for all sentient beings, and how sentient beings are suffering.

This precious living being, your baby, is one among the thousands of most kind, dear sentient beings from whom we receive all our past, present, and future happiness, realizations, and enlightenment. Of course, your child has his own karma, but both of you have full responsibility as parents to bring him up as a very good human being, full of compassion for all beings, Dharma wisdom, and all the precious qualities of the mind: a sense of universal responsibility, forgiveness, tolerance, and so on.

You can help your child develop his mind on the path by teaching him:

> ❧ **To not harm living beings, and**

> ❧ **To bring happiness to them,**

not only temporary happiness but ultimate, everlasting happiness—liberation and full enlightenment.

This precious living being, your baby, is one among the thousands of most kind, dear sentient beings from whom we receive all our past, present, and future happiness, realizations, and enlightenment.

31

Even if it is not possible to bring this to everyone, at least he can avoid harming others and can bring others some degree of happiness. That would be so wonderful. You are a very good human being, so I am sure your child will easily become one too, due to your example, inspiration, and blessing.

I will pray for his long life and health and for him to have a most beneficial life.

Thank you very much.

With much love and prayers,

REMEMBER

- It is our job to bring up our child as a good human being, full of compassion, forgiveness, and tolerance.

A Baby Is Not Just for Your Own Pleasure

Dear Lama Zopa,
My husband Norman and I are trying to decide whether to have a baby. We are not sure. On the one hand, we are concerned about the cost involved, about the time and effort raising a child requires, about the current state of the world, and about the enormous change it would mean to the way we currently live.

On the other hand, we wonder whether we are forgoing one of life's joys by not having children. It seems a little lonely and selfish not to have a child, or not to give our parents grandchildren. I am a little afraid (and I think my husband is too) of reaching old age and regretting the absence of children, of not having the comfort of a family around us.

Please, what is your advice?

Best wishes,
Jeanette, Washington, D.C.

You are a very good human being, so I am sure your child will easily become one too, due to your example, inspiration, and blessing.

Dear Jeanette and Norman,

Raising a child makes life so complicated! However, if your plan is

1. **To give a human body to a sentient being who is looking for a human body, and**

2. **To bring a child up in a way that would make his or her life most beneficial for the world,**

that is different. With *that* plan, you can manage well. If your attitude is according to that plan from the beginning, and the material side of things can be managed, it's okay.

But without that plan, then having a child is something done just for one's own pleasure, like getting a pet. Instead of increasing kindness, patience, tolerance, peace, and happiness in the world, it only increases attachment and leads to more trouble for you and the world.

I think the question of whether to have a child very much depends on what kind of life the child is likely to have.

Love and prayers,

REMEMBER

- **I need to know how to bring up a baby so that its life will be beneficial for others.**

Without that plan, then having a child is something done just for one's own pleasure, like getting a pet.

How to Bring Up a Child

Dear Lama Zopa,

My extended family is putting a lot of pressure on me and my husband to have a child. Needless to say, having a child is a tremendous responsibility, and I have seen how difficult it is to raise a child in a culture with so much violence and greed—even when the parents have the best of intentions. I have serious reservations about whether bringing another child into this world is the most beneficial thing to do, especially if the main reason is to please our families.

Rinpoche, can you please advise me about whether it is beneficial to have a child? If so, what is the best way to raise the child to be a kind and peaceful person? Thank you.

Best wishes,
Wenyu, Hong Kong

Dear Wenyu,

You should be clear about your purpose for having a child. It is to raise it with a good heart.

> ☙ Think: "I must give love and compassion, kindness, and generosity to others, and have a sense of universal responsibility—feeling responsible for all living beings' happiness."

Then there will be so much peace and happiness in your life and fulfillment in your heart. Your decision will bring great happiness to all living beings, the world, your country, and your family.

When a person is generous, good-hearted, and kind to others, then all the good things in life come from that. Such a person will enjoy prosperity, health, and a long life. If those good qualities are in a person's mind, even if he or she lives in poverty, the person will experience peace and happiness, and there will be satisfaction and fulfillment in his or her heart.

> ☙ One of the most important things in life, which is missing in schools and universities, is education in the practice of transforming our minds and actions.

Since the future peace and happiness of the world depends on the children, even if only 50 percent of them practice transforming their minds and actions, it would help very much to bring peace to their country and to the world.

Since the future peace and happiness of the world depends on the children, even if only 50 percent of them practice transforming their minds and actions, it would help very much to bring peace to their country and to the world.

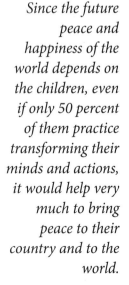

Historically, there have been individuals who have been responsible for the torture and killing of many millions of people. Conversely, you can see that if even one child or one person develops a good heart, that precious quality of the human mind, then if that person gains influence or power, he or she can bring so much peace and happiness to millions of people.

> ☙ It is very important to educate children to be kind and generous toward others, and to feel responsible for all living beings' happiness.

This kind of education is important at school and also at home. The parents also need to be educated in this way and practice a good heart, loving kindness, and compassion. They should be kind and generous to others, feel a sense of universal responsibility—a sense that they themselves are responsible for all living beings' happiness.

> ☙ According to my own divination, it would be better for you to have children than not to have them, but there is only a small benefit.

Every child has his or her own karma. How their lives will turn out depends on their previous karma and on the conditions they meet in this life. Parents are a condition, an example, and an influence on children. Many children follow their parents' ideas, behavior, and lifestyle, so parents have a great responsibility. Those who would like to have children should be aware of this. They should think about these things before they rush into having children.

With much love and prayers,

Every child has his or her own karma. How their lives will turn out depends on their previous karma and on the conditions they meet in this life. Many children follow their parents' ideas, behavior, and lifestyle, so parents have a great responsibility.

REMEMBER

- Just one person developing a good heart can bring so much happiness to the world.
- Children need to be educated, both at school and at home, in the benefits of a good heart.
- Even in poverty, if a person is generous and good-hearted, he or she will have peace and happiness.

35

What Practices to Do?

Dear Lama Zopa,
Please could you recommend practices that would be helpful in stopping the bird flu epidemic?

Best wishes,
Karen, Seattle

Dear Karen,
The practices I recommend to prevent bird flu spreading are as follows:

1. The *Mantra Purifying All Negative Karma and Defilements,*

2. *Tangtong Gyelpo's Prayer Liberating Sakya from Disease,*

3. *Black Garuda* practice,

4. *Vajra Armor mantra,* and

5. *Guru Rinpoche* prayers to clear away obstacles.

It would be very useful to do *retreat* on the Vajra Armor mantra. It doesn't have to be a strict retreat; it could also be just reciting 108 mantras a day.

With much love and prayers,

Guru Rinpoche

How to Celebrate?

Dear Lama Zopa,

How can we celebrate birthdays in a meaningful way? I get annoyed with the materialism of giving and receiving gifts. Sometimes it just feels like a chore to get through, but why should it feel this way? The years pass. This should mean something. Would you please give me some advice on how to celebrate birthdays?

Best wishes and thanks,
Dora, Adelaide

Dear Dora,
One way to celebrate a birthday is as if you have just been in a place where there was great danger but you have survived. It's a miracle!

- Think: "It's amazing that since my last birthday, over the past year, I did not die."

- Think: "It is remarkable that I have survived since birth, and that is something to celebrate."

- Think: "I have created many causes for liberation from samsara and to achieve a good rebirth in my next life, and have done many things to benefit other sentient beings."

These are worth celebrating. They are the real reason to celebrate a birthday.

If your life has been spent on meaningless or nonvirtuous activities only to achieve your own happiness for this life alone, then there's nothing in which to rejoice. If you are going to live in that way, there is no point in celebrating the future. But through realizing that, and resolving that from now on you will purify past negative actions and change your behavior, then you can celebrate.

- On the day of your birthday, you can decide to develop compassion and loving kindness for all sentient beings, including your enemies, not just those you like.

- Study the Buddha's holy deeds, and the biographies of others—not only Buddhists—who tamed their minds, subdued their egos, and only thought of cherishing others.

If your life has been spent on meaningless or nonvirtuous activities only to achieve your own happiness for this life alone, then there's nothing in which to rejoice.

Hi! all my dearest friends sentient being who are most kind, precious one. I am Twenty Century Mila repa the Englishand Tibetan Yogi. I am singing hyms for all of you, that how samsara Nirvana getting empty and bliss. I am blissed out. HA— HO. HA— HO.

Aspire to become like those beings, with their compassion and loving kindness and their renunciation, beings who, without anger, practice tolerance and contentment and have brought so much peace, happiness, and benefit to many sentient beings. If you generate that sort of wish, then you can become like those great *holy beings*. Then a birthday really becomes something to celebrate.

Many prayers,

On the day of your birthday, you can decide to develop compassion and loving kindness for all sentient beings, including your enemies, not just those you like.

REMEMBER

- There is nothing to celebrate if I use my life for meaningless activities.
- From now on I will purify my negative actions.
- I will try to become like the holy beings who have benefited others. Then I will have something to celebrate!

Why Can't I Have a Baby?

Dear Lama Zopa,
I have been married for more than twelve years, but have not been able
to have a child. My husband and I love each other very much, and I have
been examined and tested by doctors. According to Western medicine,
I seem to have no biological problems. According to Chinese medicine,
there is something cold in my physiology, and I have been taking Chinese
medicine to address this. I thought that by correcting the physical side of
the problem, conception should have occurred naturally.
Please help me understand why children are not coming to us.
Love and many thanks,
Cynthia, Taiwan

Dear Cynthia,
Besides the physical conditions, there is karma. Without having
created karma in the past—which is a thought, an intention, a mental
phenomenon—you cannot conceive. Everything depends on karma. The
existence of the whole world depends on having previously created the
cause. Even physical factors are just a condition. It is not enough to fix
the body. You need to have the karma to have a child.

Also, the child, the living being who is going to be born to you
has to have the karma. Normally, the gathering of a family is based on
having created karma in the past.

Jambhala

1. It may be good to keep a *Jambhala* statue in your
   house; he is an embodiment of Compassion Buddha.

2. You need to have a *wealth vase* made.

3. You put the statue in the vase together with many
   jewels, money, precious things, and medicine. The vase
   and deity need to be blessed.

4. Then you request Jambhala to give you a child. Do this
   every day for some time.

5. The other thing that is common among Tibetans is to
   sponsor a monastery to do Green *Tara* practice.

You can start first with these. If conception doesn't take place
within six months, many other techniques can be explored.

Love and prayers,

Everything
depends on karma.
The existence of
the whole world
depends on having
previously created
the cause.

Benefit Others

····· *Rinpoche gave this advice to the children at a school run by the FPMT in Bodhgaya, India.*

You should think that the purpose of going to school and getting an education is so you can benefit all living beings.

Parents Are the Main Educators

Dear Lama Zopa,
My wife and I are blessed with two wonderful children, but I am worried about how best to raise them. I am a Buddhist practitioner, but far from a buddha! How should we educate them in the home? What is the best way to encourage them to lead positive and happy lives? Should we use discipline or only gentleness? These are hard choices, especially when our love for them is admittedly polluted by attachment.

Your advice will be greatly appreciated.

Your student,
Jim, Chicago

Dear Jim,
Educating children is extremely important. There are two places where children should be educated: at school and at home.

> ➤ **They should be educated in having a good heart, tolerance, compassion, and being kind to others. These are the basic good qualities of the human mind, so parents have a big responsibility.**

Without this education, it is like giving birth to suffering. The children will have a life full of suffering, and they will also give so much suffering to their parents and other people. They will cause other sentient beings many problems with their untamed minds, without a good heart and a sense of universal responsibility.

If children have tolerance and compassion for other beings, other beings will love them and help them.

> ➤ **Think: "If I want my children to be kind to me, I have to teach them how to have a good heart."**

If children have tolerance and compassion for other beings, other beings will love them and help them. Having a good heart will make them happy, and then they will have more space in their minds to be kind to others, and this will make others happy.

Parents are a stronger influence than school because children spend more time with them, and the way of teaching is by example. In school, you learn by the head and not the heart. What is needed is an education for parents and children alike in having a good heart.

Love and prayers,

REMEMBER

- **Without a good heart, a child's life creates nothing but suffering for themselves, their parents, and others.**

Growing Up Too Fast

Dear Lama Zopa,
I have a sixteen-year-old daughter, and I am worried about our relationship and the direction she is headed in. She seems to be growing up way too fast, which causes me great concern; she stays out late, runs with an older crowd, and I think she isn't always truthful with me about what she is doing. I have tried setting limits on her behavior, but she breaks the rules. I have tried being gentle, but then she walks all over me. I have tried yelling, but then she completely shuts down.

How do I correct her direction? I am terrified that she is going to do something she'll regret the rest of her life, but I seem to have lost control over her. What can I do?

Love and thanks,
Emma, Darwin

Dear Emma,
Raising children in a society full of negative influences, where bad friends are many and good friends—disciplined, compassionate friends—are few, is not easy. Just like *tsatsa* molds, our friends are like molds for us.

Parents are a stronger influence than school because children spend more time with them, and the way of teaching is by example.

41

Western culture is filled with so much desire. It is not like so-called less-developed places. In the West, advertisements are all about desire and what to do to best satisfy our desire; for instance, food commercials make us want to eat. Such messages in our environment can have a powerful effect on us. And all these things—bad friends, the culture, conditions at school—make teenagers uneasy.

- **Teach your child never to forget about karma.**

- **Every day, pray to Medicine Buddha that your child will grow up with all the qualities of the buddhas—of Tara and of Chenrezig—with the best attributes.**

The prayers of people who share a home have great power for each other.

If you just pray for a healthy life for your daughter and for other things like that, then you are just focusing on the benefits of this life. That is not so good. Pray instead that she may develop all the best inner qualities, and can then be free from suffering and can help all sentient beings.

With much love and prayers,

The prayers of people who share a home have great power for each other.

REMEMBER

- It is not enough to just want my daughter to be healthy. I must pray for her long-term happiness.

Is It Possible to See the Future?

Dear Lama Zopa,
I've heard that the Buddhist teachings say that all minds have the power to develop clairvoyance. How is that possible? And how might one use such a skill? Please let me know your thoughts, Rinpoche.

Best wishes,
Peter, Santa Cruz

Dear Peter,
Because some people have a clear mind, which is less polluted and obscured, they can see things happening that other people cannot see, and are even able to see things in distant countries.

Some people can remember being in their mother's womb and being born. I know one person who has a clear memory of that. Even though most people don't remember, many do.

> ☙ Also, there are so many children who can remember their past lives and describe them very clearly. This is not just the experience of Tibetan lamas; there are people in the West who are born with a clear memory of past lives.

The great saints, the arya bodhisattvas, can see millions of past and future lives.

Through developing meditation, especially the meditation of *calm abiding,* the mind becomes more clear and one can develop higher powers.

> ☙ One is able to see the past and future through meditation on a *deity* as well. One can even achieve this by reciting mantras such as *Om mani padme hum.*

The whole thing is a question of how clear the mind is. The less polluted or defiled the mind, the more capacity one has to see the past, present, and future, which most people don't have the clarity or capacity to see. This is the potential of the mind that can be developed: the clarity of mind that can clearly remember past lives and future lives.

> ☙ I think the United States and other countries need to develop clairvoyance, the power of seeing beyond what ordinary people know, which is very limited, so that they can use it to protect lives.

The great saints, the arya bodhisattvas, can see millions of past and future lives.

The syllable **Hum**

However, even if the clairvoyance is highly developed, it is still not possible to prevent all destructive, dangerous situations. But with the power to see beyond what ordinary people see, you would have the capacity to prevent many great harms. Consider the events of September 11th, for example. The terrorists had been studying and practicing for a number of years, and finally they committed the act, which was their aim. Everything had been disguised. If you were able to read their minds, you would know their ideas and plans.

External protection is limited. The power to see the minds of others can help us do more to protect the lives of others.

With much love and prayers,

With the power to see beyond what ordinary people see, you would have the capacity to prevent many great harms.

REMEMBER

• **It is possible to develop clairvoyance.**

What to Do?

Dear Lama Zopa,

There are many cockroaches in our Buddhist center. We certainly do not want to kill them, but we would like to be free of them! Whenever we have teachings, they can be seen and heard scurrying about. A number of people have complained, and we are afraid their presence may alienate members. What do you recommend?

Best wishes,
Chodron, New Mexico

Dear Chodron,

There is a reason why they have come to the center. It's because you have a karmic debt with them. They didn't come intentionally; it's not like all the cockroaches had a meeting and decided to move into the center; it happened by the force of karma.

There are a few things you can do.

1. Perform the *sur offering* for them and the *hundred-torma offering*.

This will repay your karmic debt with them. If you didn't have a karmic debt with them, they wouldn't come. It's the same with mice or insects that eat crops and flowers, or woodworm in a house.

2. Offer them what they want, offer charity to them.

This is a great opportunity to offer things to sentient beings.

3. Talk to the cockroaches and ask them to leave.

One of my students spoke to a mouse and asked it to move outside the house and it went. There are other stories like that.

4. Put the cockroaches in a small part of the house; or make a house out of a paper box, find out what they like to eat, and put it in the box; then, after they have gone into the box, put the box outside.

Then, sometimes, go and give them food. By putting them in the box they are protected. Giving food regularly becomes an act of charity.

With much love and prayers,

It's not like all the cockroaches had a meeting and decided to move into the center; it happened by the force of karma.

REMEMBER

• Giving food regularly becomes an act of charity.

Karma Is More Powerful When Created by Many

Dear Lama Zopa,
I am hoping you can help me with some questions I have about karma.
In particular, I am very disturbed about all the killing taking place in the
world and am trying to understand the karmic implications. When there
is a lot of popular support for killing, as with capital punishment and war,
who is it that receives the karma? Does only the person directly responsible
for the killing receive the karma, or does everybody share in it? If everyone
shares the karma, is it diluted? In other words, does group karma mean
that an individual's share is less than for actions done independently?
Thanks and best wishes,
Donna, Wisconsin

Dear Donna,
Karma is more powerful when it is created by many people. For example, if one hundred people all established the intention to kill a sheep and then killed a sheep, each one of these people would have the negative karma of killing that sheep.

This means that

- If a government makes the decision to go to war and they are supported by the population of that country, each person will receive the karma of killing, however many people die.

If one human being is killed, everyone will receive the karma of killing one human being. If a thousand people are killed, everyone will receive the karma of having killed a thousand people.

But if one person kills a sheep without the support of other people, only that person will get the negative karma of having killed one sheep. If you compare to see which karma is more powerful, the previous instance, where many people had the same intention and then killed a sheep, is more powerful.

Similarly,

- Whether one hundred people build a stupa or just one person builds a stupa, the merit each person collects is the same. Thus there is much more merit if many people build the stupa.

Similarly, if you compare the karma of one sangha person—a monk or nun—reciting a *sutra* once in a temple or room without any other support, or reciting a sutra with all the assembly of sangha, the latter—reciting the sutra with all the sangha—is much more powerful.

This applies to reciting prayers like *Guru Puja* alone, either in one's own room or in the temple, or with a group. Reciting it in a group is more powerful. The more people that support the practice, the more powerful it becomes.

When karma is more powerful, the result comes more quickly, whether the goal is a project or realization.

Love and prayers,

REMEMBER

- The more people who support an action, the greater the karma that results.
- When karma is more powerful, the result comes more quickly.

Karma is more powerful when it is created by many people.

The Government Took My Money

Dear Lama Zopa,

I married a very wealthy man who owned a large company. I tried to use the money to help poor, sick people, and often paid hospital bills for people who couldn't afford them.

My husband died in 1978. At the time, the president of our country (I don't live there any more) appropriated the company's funds, saying that the government needed one billion U.S. dollars and would repay it later. This was our family's money and was supposed to be divided among us, according to my husband's will. It's not likely we will ever get it back.

What do you advise, Rinpoche?

Best wishes,
Patty, Australia

Dear Patty,

> ✦ **You can try rejoicing that the president and the government got the money.**

Rejoicing in the good fortune of others is an easy way to create merit. One billion dollars is such a huge amount that if you rejoice, you receive an enormous amount of merit. With more merit, you will be able to make more money. You might make even more money than was lost.

> ✦ **Think: "Even the earth will be empty one day; none of this will exist any more. We will have to leave everything, including our body, our family, relations, and possessions—everything."**

We have to separate from them one day. Even if the government hadn't taken the money, at the time of your death it would have to be left behind. Death and this separation can happen any time.

Life is not long. Only a small number of people live for one hundred years. It's better to have a happy, positive mind toward one another. Looking at this situation in a positive way is good, because it makes you happy. If you are happy, you can make everyone else happy.

With much love and prayers,

Looking at this situation in a positive way is good, because it makes you happy. If you are happy, you can make everyone else happy.

REMEMBER

- I can look at this situation in a positive way.
- I can't take it with me when I die anyway.

It Is Not God's Fault

Dear Lama Zopa,
My father died suddenly in the morning, just a few days ago. My family has not taken it well. They all seem to blame God and are angry with God for taking our father away. Their anger has thrown me into confusion. How should I think of my father's sudden death?

Love and best wishes,
Tony, Singapore

My very dear Tony,
It is not God's fault. It is your father's karma to pass away. Life is not permanent. The Buddha said that it is impermanent in nature. That is the reality we experience. It is also not Buddha's fault.

The most important thing is that your father didn't die in much pain. It is good that it happened suddenly. We should pray for him to have a good rebirth in his next life, to be born in a *pure land* where he can become enlightened (or you can say, where he can be with God), or receive a perfect human rebirth so he can achieve enlightenment in that life by meeting a qualified spriritual teacher and putting the Mahayana teachings into practice correctly.

> Think: "We are all on the same journey as my father. This is the reality of life."

It is very important to realize this and remember it every day. The benefit of doing this is that we prepare for death and happiness in our future lives. More important than this is liberation from samsara, which is called *nirvana*. Most important of all is achieving enlightenment for the benefit of all sentient beings. The only way is through Dharma practice: pure mind and pure action.

> Think: "I can help my father by performing many virtuous actions and dedicating the merits to him."

This way, you can still help him, so please be happy!

With much love and prayer,

We should pray for him to have a good rebirth in his next life, to be born in a pure land where he can become enlightened (or, you can say, where he can be with God).

REMEMBER

- **Life is not permanent: thinking about this is the way to prepare for my own death.**

You Must Tell a Person They Are Dying

Dear Lama Zopa,
My sister Kerry has been diagnosed with advanced cancer. She has exhausted the options for a cure, and the doctors have told us she is nearing death. We are concerned about her state of mind and are reluctant to tell her that she will die soon. We would like her to be able to spend her last days peacefully and to make the best use of the time left. But is it right not to tell her? Some members of the family and I myself feel we should tell her that she is going to die soon.

Love,
Nancy, Santa Fe

Dear Nancy,
It is not appropriate to withhold this important and relevant information from her. Knowing that she only has a very short time to live should help her make what time *is* left most useful. This is very critical for her.

The main thing for her is to practice compassion. Always keep this in mind.

> She should keep repeating: "I am going to die for the benefit of all sentient beings. The practice, the service, that I am doing and have done is for the benefit of sentient beings."

I have sponsored prayers to be done for her. They are all for the purpose of her purification and good rebirth, and she should not worry. This is what I am saying to her.

With much love and prayers,

Knowing that she only has a very short time to live should help her make what time is left most useful.

The Best Way to Die

Dear Lama Zopa,
What practices should I perform if I know I am about to die?
Love,
Tom, California

Dear Tom,

1. **Generally speaking, practice bodhichitta. That's the safest one.**

2. **However, for somebody who has good concentration, there is meditation on emptiness.**

If a person has realized emptiness, then he or she sees as a hallucination—as false—anything that appears real from its own side and appears not to be merely labeled by the mind.

That helps. How? Because whether you try to look at something as empty or not, when you see it as false, and understand that it *is* false, that makes you realize there is no reason to cling to or get angry about something. Meditation on emptiness protects the mind from delusions and from creating negative karma so that you don't die with anger or attachment.

Ultimately, though, in order not to be reborn in the lower realms, or in order not to be reborn at all, you have to cut the root of samsara.

With much love and prayers,

REMEMBER

- **Seeing something as false helps realize there is nothing to cling to or get angry about.**

How to Help at Death

Dear Lama Zopa,

I am writing you with some sad and urgent news. We recently found out that my mother's lung cancer is terminal; she does not have much longer to live. Maybe due to the fact that my wife and I have been practicing Buddhism for the last twenty years, my mother developed an interest in the Dharma late in life. She does not have any kind of formal practice but has asked me to write to you for advice about what she can do before she dies. We would be grateful for any guidance about what she can do in her final days.

Love and thanks,
Jack, Florida

Meditation on emptiness protects the mind from delusions and from creating negative karma so that you don't die with anger or attachment.

Dear Jack,

1. **Place a picture of Tara so she can die looking at it.**

2. **Play CDs of mantras constantly for her until she dies.**

3. **Ask someone to read *The Heart Sutra* and prayers to her so she can hear them before she dies.**

With much love and prayers,

····· *Rinpoche also went to the hospital to visit the student's mother and to bless her. Later, Jack's mother died with her eyes open, facing the image of Tara that Rinpoche had given her. The resident teacher at the Dharma center where she was a member visited her the night before she died and commented that no one would be afraid of dying if they could see her. The woman was calm and upbeat as she said goodbye to people the day before she died. One of the last things she told her son was that it was all very clear, and that she felt good.*

How to Die Well

Dear Lama Zopa,
Our dear friend Mary, who is a Buddhist, is dying. She is moving back and forth between consciousness and unconsciousness. How can we help her die well?

Ann and Joey,
Madison, Wisconsin.

One of the last things she told her son was that it was all very clear, and that she felt good.

Dearest Ann and Joey,
Tell Mary that I have done prayers for her in front of Buddha's relics. I did the dedication already and will pray again.

There are several things you can help her do.

1. Whenever Mary wakes up, it's good for her to think in this way:

- Think: "The purpose of my life is not only my own happiness, and not only solving my own problems. The goal of my life is to free others from suffering and to cause all the happiness, temporal and ultimate, for others."

- Think: "I'm just one living being. My importance is nothing. How much I suffer or how much happiness I achieve is nothing. There are numberless other living beings who want happiness, who don't want suffering, and who need my help."

- Think: "Every one of them is the source of all my past, present, and future happiness. Each of them is the most precious one in my life."

- Think: "How very fortunate I am that I can let go of my self—from which all problems and all the undesirable things come—and instead cherish others and experience all their deaths and all their problems for them, and let them have all the temporal and ultimate happiness."

- She should imagine that she breathes in all their suffering in the form of smoke, and that it destroys the ego. The ego becomes nonexistent.

*His Holiness
the Dalai Lama*

2. She should have near her a picture of Medicine Buddha and a very nice photo of His Holiness the Dalai Lama, with a very happy, joyful, blissful expression.

3. You can tell her to pray from time to time throughout the day, while looking at a picture of His Holiness. He's the Compassion Buddha, the embodiment of all buddhas' compassion in human form. Tell her to think that this is his nature, and that therefore he loves her. His compassion embraces her all the time. She should think that.

4. She can also look at Medicine Buddha's picture, remembering him. If she dies with the thought of Medicine Buddha, she will never get reborn in the suffering lower realms. Even just by hearing the Medicine Buddha's name and mantra, she has no need to be afraid of death.

When she prays to them, she can

- Think: "From now on, in all my future lives, may I become like them, having *perfect complete wisdom, perfect complete compassion,* and *perfect complete power* to offer numberless benefits as vast as the sky

*If she dies with
the thought of
Medicine Buddha,
she will never
get reborn in the
suffering lower
realms.*

toward all sentient beings. May I become like this from now on, and in all my future lifetimes."

5. At the time of death, if it's possible, she should

- Lie down in the same position as the position in which Buddha passed away into the sorrowless state. This is called the position of a snow lion sleeping. Lying on her right side, the right cheek rests on the right hand, and the left hand rests on top of the thigh. Normally, too, the ring finger of the right hand is bent and rests on the upper lip. This is to stop the *wind* of attachment, not to die with the thought of attachment. It is due to attachment that one remains caught in samsara.

Dying in this physical position will help her to die with virtuous thoughts. And if she can think of how Buddha passed away, that helps to remember Buddha.

6. Then there is the way to prepare for death mentally, for dying the correct way—not only the correct way, but the beneficial way. There are thoughts for making even death—our last experience in life—beneficial for others, which is the most critical thing. Tell her to try to die with the thought:

- "I'm experiencing death on behalf of all sentient beings. I'm unbelievably lucky to be able to experience my death for others, for the happiness of numberless living beings, to free them from suffering. I'm unbelievably lucky to be able to use my death to achieve peerless happiness, full enlightenment, to use it to bring every one to the highest happiness of full enlightenment."

Dying with the thought of others is the best way of dying. All the buddhas and bodhisattvas, all the holy beings, will admire you. It will make them so happy that you are dying with this thought.

Dying with the thought of others is the best way of dying. All the buddhas and bodhisattvas, all the holy beings, will admire you. It will make them so happy that you are dying with this thought. This is the best path for you to open the door to all happiness. This way, there's no suffering; there are no difficulties at the time of death. Dying like this, there is no fear, and there will be no lower rebirth.

7. Or she could die with the thought of His Holiness the Dalai Lama. When there are signs that death is nearing, when the breath starts to become stronger out than in, for example, or when the nostrils become flat and the eyes roll and become larger—these are signs that death may be one hour to an hour and a half away—she can do the following meditation. Actually, she can practice this meditation from time to time throughout the day, in preparation for death:

- Visualize His Holiness above her crown. Beams of light come from His Holiness's heart chakra, enter her crown, and go down her *central channel* to her heart chakra. Now the channel is no longer hollow, and the opening below the heart chakra is closed. Her consciousness is inside, the size of a mustard seed and in the nature of white light.

- Then red beams emit from His Holiness the Dalai Lama's heart to her consciousness, and the red beams hook her consciousness and bring it to His Holiness's heart.

- Then her consciousness becomes one with His Holiness the Dalai Lama. She feels oneness with His Holiness's holy mind, which has the nature of great bliss, infinite bliss. She should feel this as long as she can.

This is for her to do. Then there are things both of you can do.

1. You should make a Shakyamuni Buddha tsatsa and a tsatsa of a stupa, with mantras inside. Do it soon so she can keep it with her.

2. It may be difficult for her to practice at the time of death, so it will be very helpful for you to say the Dalai Lama's name or Medicine Buddha's mantra in her ear.

3. As death approaches, make sure her body is in the snow-lion position.

4. Before the breath stops, place pills made of butter and sand from the *Kalachakra mandala* on the crown of her head. These pills should be made ahead of time.

5. Once the breath stops, do not touch her until the heat is gone from her body. It is extremely important that when she *is* touched, it should first be on the crown of her head. You can pull her hair at the crown, tugging it, before the doctors and nurse come and touch her. This can help her consciousness leave through her crown, which can indicate a good rebirth.

With much love and prayer,

Once the breath stops, do not touch her until the heat is gone from her body.

REMEMBER

- Dying with the thought of the Medicine Buddha, I never go to the lower realms.
- Dying with the thought of benefiting others is the most meaningful way to die.
- His Holiness the Dalai Lama is the Compassion Buddha.

Advice at the Time of Execution

····· *Below are excerpts from an eighteen-page letter that Rinpoche wrote to a prisoner in Texas, newly Buddhist, who had just been given his date of execution for three months' time. (Ted's execution has twice been delayed; the Supreme Court's decision will be announced before July 2007.)*

My very dear Ted,

Here are some things for you to think about, some suggestions about how to use your situation, and the best things you can do, the most practical things left for you to practice.

Even if you only have one day left to live, or one hour, you still have an incredible opportunity to make your human body—which you have received just this one time—most beneficial. Even someone with only one hour left can still, in that time, take the *five lay vows* or the *eight Mahayana precepts.*

The Best Practices for You

1. **Lay vows: It would be best for you to take the life-long lay vows as soon as possible, however many you can keep: No killing, no lying, no stealing, no *sexual misconduct,* no drugs or alcohol. Until then you can also take the eight Mahayana precepts, which are taken for twenty-four hours at a time.**

2. **Meditate on Chenrezig and recite his mantra: Here is a photo of a Chenrezig painting that I always carry with me on my travels. According to my divinations, it is best for you to do the practice of Chenrezig, the Compassion Buddha.**

Visualize Chenrezig in front of you. As you recite the mantra, *Om mani padme hum,* visualize nectar coming out from Chenrezig and entering you and purifying all your sicknesses, negative karma, spirit harms, and defilements. For half the *mala* rosary, visualize being purified, and for the other half visualize that you receive all the qualities of Chenrezig. Chenrezig completely embraces all sentient beings and knows directly all sentient beings' minds, all the methods to guide them perfectly, with perfect power, perfect wisdom, and perfect compassion.

3. ***Thought transformation:* Transformation by Langri Tangpa is very important. Meditate on the verses and**

Even someone with only one hour left can still, in that time, take the five lay vows or the eight Mahayana precepts.

recite *Om mani padme hum* after each verse. At the end, feel extremely happy because you are practicing and generating bodhichitta, the thought to benefit others.

4. Meditate on emptiness, as well, to realize how the "I," *aggregates,* and phenomena are empty of existence from their own side; that they exist in mere name, merely imputed by the mind.

5. *Lamrim prayer:* It is very good if you can read a complete lamrim prayer every day, such as *The Foundation of All Good Qualities.* Each time that you read this, it plants a seed for the whole path to enlightenment in your mind and makes your life extremely worthwhile.

Here is a photo of a Chenrezig painting that I always carry with me on my travels.

6. *Marichi* mantra: It would be very good for you to recite three hundred Marichi mantras every day.

Practices on the Day of Your Execution:
Thought Transformation and Bodhichitta

1. On the day that you will be executed, the last thing to do before you are executed is to take complete refuge in Chenrezig. Think of Chenrezig, visualize the picture I sent you, and totally rely on Chenrezig.

2. Think: "May I experience all the suffering of all beings who have the karma to be executed and of those who actually perform the execution, and may I let everyone else be free from this suffering."

3. Put your palms together in the *mudra* of prostration to Chenrezig and request to be guided by Chenrezig in all future lifetimes until enlightenment.

4. Think: "May I receive all sentient beings' karma to be executed, may I experience this by myself alone, and because of that may all others be free from all sufferings and receive all peerless happiness up to enlightenment."

5. Continuously think this way, over and over again.

It is incredibly powerful if you die with this thought of giving yourself up to experience all other beings' suffering of being executed and giving all your happiness to others. This becomes your main refuge. In particular, feel this for those who have the job of executing you, as well as the people who have given this order, the judge, and so on. By their creating this negative karma, then having acted on it—which comes from an impure mind, attachment, anger, *ignorance,* and, particularly, the self-cherishing thought—they will have to experience the karma of being executed by others for five hundred lifetimes, just from this one action of killing, which is the cause.

If you die with a nonvirtuous thought, a self-cherishing thought, of ignorance, anger, or attachment, then you will be reborn in the animal, hungry ghost, or hell realms. While you are in the lower realms, you continually create more negative karma, which will result in again being reborn in the lower realms. Even spending one day in the lower realms collects so much negative karma, the ten nonvirtues, and so forth.

It is incredibly powerful if you die with the thought of giving yourself up to experience all other beings' suffering of being executed and giving all your happiness to others.

It is very beneficial if you die with the thought of benefiting other sentient beings. It is the best way to die, the best quality death. You are dying for all those other living beings, which means you are not dying for yourself. This is similar to Jesus, who took on the suffering of other sentient beings, or Shakyamuni Buddha, who in a previous life offered his body to a starving tigress and her five cubs; he gave up his life because he could not bear their suffering.

> ● Using this punishment of being executed as a means to achieve enlightenment for sentient beings becomes the cause of happiness for all sentient beings—not just temporal happiness, but liberation from samsara and ultimate happiness, full enlightenment.

Therefore, there is no greater happiness than this. Your execution is an opportunity to bring ultimate joy and happiness to yourself and all other sentient beings.

Happiness and problems all depend on your interpretation, on your labeling them "happiness" and "problems," and then your believing in the label: only then do experiences actually become suffering or happiness. Training in being able to transform your execution by seeing it as beneficial and a cause of happiness for all sentient beings becomes a great challenge. What is suffering for most people can be transformed into great happiness for you and others. By doing this you become a champion. This is such an incredible way of thinking.

Being in Prison Is Actually an Incredible Opportunity

Another way is to rejoice: if you were not in prison your mind would be so distracted, disturbed, and preoccupied by objects of attachment, anger, and so forth. You would have no time to meditate and no interest in spiritual practice because your life would be so busy and occupied with the objects of desire.

> ● Think: "By being in prison I have an incredible opportunity. It has helped me to awaken my mind, to analyze myself, and to think about my own life."

This makes being in prison very profound. Being in this situation, you feel very deeply the wish to actualize the spiritual path and to meditate. Therefore, your life in prison is actually much happier than an ordinary life outside prison, especially now that you know about karma, how suffering comes from the mind, and how the mind is the main cause.

By knowing this you can have a happy life, happy death, and

Happiness and problems all depend on your interpretation, on your labeling them "happiness" and "problems," and then your believing in the label.

happy rebirth, by purifying negative karma and creating good karma, virtuous actions. Not only that, you discover there is a much deeper achievement in life: ultimate happiness and liberation from samsara (the circling again and again from one life to the next, the continuity of the aggregates caused by karma and delusion, the contamination by the seed of delusion, all the sufferings and their causes) by realizing the *four noble truths*—the true cause of suffering, true suffering, true cessation of suffering, and the true path. You can discover that there is an opportunity to learn the true path and to achieve this by listening, reflecting, and meditating. As long we do not eliminate the causes of suffering—the deluded mind and its actions—we will have to reincarnate and die and experience all the sufferings in between over and over without end.

What most people in the world believe is suffering is very limited. What they want to be liberated from is just the extremely gross sufferings. But there is so much suffering that they are not aware of. Ignorance blocks them from achieving total liberation and from seeking the true path. Ignorance also blocks them from finding the worldly happiness that they are looking for—which is actually a kind of suffering, not happiness—and even the method to achieve the happiness that they want. They are only looking outside themselves for happiness, and that is why their lives are continually drawn into suffering, from life to life.

> ♣ **Therefore, being in prison is extremely positive, a great advantage and joy. You have an incredible opportunity: to have happiness now, a happy death, happy future lives, happy liberation from samsara, and happy great liberation: full enlightenment.**

What most people in the world believe is suffering is very limited. What they want to be liberated from is just the extremely gross sufferings. But there is so much suffering that they are not aware of.

Experiencing the Suffering of Others Causes Happiness for Oneself

> ♣ **If one gives up one's life for others, experiences their suffering, and gives one's happiness to others, instead of causing suffering for oneself, it actually causes the opposite of suffering; it causes happiness.**

Recently, in Seattle, a woman had cancer that had spread all over her body. The doctors were afraid to do an operation; they felt that it was too risky and dangerous. So she did the bodhichitta practice of tonglen, taking on sentient beings' sufferings and the causes of suffering, and giving one's own merits and happiness to others, exchanging oneself for others. After some time, when she went to the hospital for a check-up, they did not find any cancer. The doctors were completely amazed, they could not understand how this meditation could totally cure her cancer. This is one subject that they cannot explain. This is one of the benefits of practicing bodhichitta, letting go of the "I," and cherishing others.

> ☙ This is why I am saying that you can use the situation of being in prison, being executed, as a means to develop bodhichitta, exchanging yourself for others. Instead of cherishing the "I," cherish others; instead of giving to oneself, give to others.

This is said in the teachings of Buddha, but also this is the reality that you can see in your own life, from your own experiences. Global problems, problems in a country, family problems, individual problems—all these problems come from cherishing the "I."

> ☙ By cherishing the "I" one opens the door to all sufferings. By cherishing others one opens the door to all happiness, inner peace, joy, satisfaction, and fulfillment right now in your heart.

You are able to overcome all the problems in your life and your mind; you will have a very happy death, a self-directed death, as well as happy future lives, and, especially, ultimate happiness, total liberation from all suffering and its causes, and enlightenment. Cherishing others is the cause of temporal and ultimate happiness for all sentient beings up to enlightenment.

The Real Prison

Worldly people believe that prison has a beginning and an end. But the real prison is being under the control of delusion and its action, karma—being caught, enveloped, trapped in this samsaric prison, these aggregates, which continually cycle from one life to another, without a second's break. This prison is caused by karma and the contaminated seed of delusion. Because of that, these aggregates, which are in the nature of pervasive, compounded suffering, become the cause to experience both the suffering of pain and the suffering of change. The suffering of change is temporary samsaric pleasure, which is in the nature of suffering because it does not last. This pleasure is something we project onto the base, which is suffering. That is why samsaric pleasures do not last, why you don't have pleasure all the time. Even pleasure is in the nature of impermanence, is decaying minute by minute, second by second. It doesn't last for even a minute or a second.

These aggregates are the real prison, which has no beginning.

As long we do not eliminate the causes of suffering—the deluded mind and its actions—we will have to reincarnate and die and experience all the sufferings in between over and over again without end.

61

DEATH ROW

We have been enmeshed in this from time without beginning. We have experienced so many hell-realm sufferings, hungry-ghost sufferings, animal sufferings, human sufferings, *devas'* sufferings, and *asuras'* sufferings, from time without beginning. It doesn't end until we actualize the path by realizing that it is suffering, by realizing the true cause of suffering, and by achieving the cessation of all the sufferings and their causes. This is the most terrifying prison, this is the real prison that we should try to be free from, right away, without delaying for even a second.

We are caught in this, and continuously we suffer. But not only that: so many sentient beings have to suffer for us, for our comfort, so that we can survive. So many other beings have to die and harm others so that we can enjoy shelter. So many sentient beings in the soil died when our house was built. So many beings had to suffer for our comfort and pleasure, for us to survive. So many sentient beings had to die so that we could eat and drink; others had to create negative karma by killing; there are so many hardships. It is similar with our clothing: so many beings had to be killed, or created the cause of killing—harming others—in order to make our clothing. Also, when we travel, so many beings die when we drive a car, so many beings get crushed. So, you can see, being caught in samsara is the most frightening thing; one can't stand it even for one second.

> → Therefore, one must listen to, reflect on, and meditate on the path; one must practice on the path that has been revealed by the wise, compassionate, kind, omniscient one, Guru Shakyamuni Buddha.

Only through this can one be liberated from samsara so that other sentient beings don't have to suffer for you, don't have to create negative karma for you, don't have to harm others for you. You can see that one has the responsibility not only to liberate oneself but to liberate many sentient beings from this samsaric prison as well.

> → You can make your life in prison very meaningful, even achieve enlightenment.

This is an incredible opportunity, a retreat away from the inner prison, being controlled by the self-cherishing thought, ignorance, anger, attachment, and negative emotional thoughts. You can achieve not only temporary happiness but create the cause to obtain ultimate happiness, liberation from samsara, and the peerless happiness of full enlightenment. You can do this while you are in your living space, which is labeled by ordinary people as prison.

So many sentient beings have to suffer for us, for our comfort, so that we can survive.

➤ Now you can feel incredible joy at being in prison, and you can see how to make your life so meaningful. If you do these practices, all the buddhas and bodhisattvas will be with you, around you, supporting you; all the holy beings will be with you when you die.

Thank you very much and with much love and prayers,

REMEMBER

- It is very beneficial if I die with the thought of benefiting other sentient beings.
- Happiness and problems all depend on how my mind interprets them.
- Ignorance blocks me from achieving liberation and from seeking the true path.
- To stop taking suffering rebirths and to take happy rebirths, I must practice Dharma and purify past negative karma.
- I must use this time in prison to practice meditation and Dharma.

This is an incredible opportunity, a retreat away from the inner prison, being controlled by the self-cherishing thought, ignorance, anger, attachment, and negative emotional thoughts.

My Friend Owes Me Money

Dear Lama Zopa,
A friend of mine, another woman, borrowed money from me a while
ago. She has not paid me back and I have let the matter slide, giving her
more and more time. Now I have stopped working in order to do Dharma
practice and probably have less money than she does. I am about to start
a three-year retreat and I need the money. How should I deal with my
friend?

> *Love,*
> *Caitlin, San Jose*

Dear Caitlin,
I suggest

> ✒ **You ask the person owing you the money to return**
> **as much as he or she is able, since now there is an**
> **important reason for the money to be returned.**

Then, whatever amount he or she is unable to repay you, in your mind
you should make an offering of that amount to the person, as an act of
charity.

This is the practice of the bodhisattvas.

With much love and prayers,

Whatever amount
he or she is unable
to repay you, in
your mind make
an offering of that
amount to the
person, as an act
of charity. This is
the practice of the
bodhisattvas.

Transforming Depression

Dear Lama Zopa,

Over the past three years, I have experienced periods of deep depression. First, it was due to a divorce. Since then, I have moved to a new city, made a new life and career, and still I feel like I can't shake the depression. It's always in the background, like a low-grade fever, and from time to time it comes up more strongly. I have tried the usual approaches—psychotherapy, antidepressants—but I still can't seem to get to the bottom of it. There are times when the depression comes and there doesn't seem to be a real reason. Yet still it's there.

Please advise me, Rinpoche. I feel like I have tried everything.

Love,

Elizabeth, Montana

Dear Elizabeth,

Thank you so much for your email.

At the beginning it is good to accept your depression, thinking, "I created the cause for this in a past life." That will help.

> ☙ **Use the depression as a meditation to develop renunciation of samsara, bodhichitta, and emptiness.**

This way you use your depression to free yourself of it forever. This is the long-term view. Your depression can then become the best Dharma practice, and the best way of healing yourself.

Usually, taking medicine and following psychological advice don't eliminate the karmic causes of depression, which were created in past lives, although they may ease the symptoms for a while. But in the end, when the medication is gone from the body, the problem is still there. For a long-term solution, you need purification, merit, and insight.

If you feel depressed due to a particular reason, for example, a relationship problem, meditate on that situation. If your depression seems without reason, then practice the meditation I explain here.

> ☙ **Use your depression by experiencing it with compassion. Meditate that you are taking on all sentient beings' depression and suffering, and the causes of that suffering. It comes to you and dissolves into your heart.**

In this way, you use your depression to achieve happiness, like transforming snake venom into medicine.

65

In this way, your self-cherishing thought is destroyed. Even the inherently existent "I" becomes nonexistent, the "I" that appears as if it were truly existent.

Perform this practice with compassion for others who are more depressed than you. Countless beings experience depression for many lifetimes, without end.

- Think: "I am just one living being. No matter how much suffering I experience, others, who are countless, have so much more suffering."

- Think: "By my experiencing this depression, they are free of all suffering and enjoy happiness, up until liberation and enlightenment. I am experiencing depression for them. How wonderful that I am able to do this, because all my happiness is due to the kindness of other sentient beings. They are the most precious things in my life; I receive all my happiness from them."

Then generate loving kindness for other beings:

- Think: "I must enable them to experience happiness and the cause of happiness. I offer whatever they want and need, and visualize all their happiness becoming the happiness of the pure land of the Buddha, where no problems exist."

- Think: "They receive the purest, highest sense pleasures, enjoyments, and beauty from me—everything they need. This causes them to actualize the whole path to enlightenment. All beings become enlightened in this way."

Perform this meditation—taking suffering and giving happiness in this way—five, ten, twenty times or more, if possible, in the morning, afternoon, and evening. Spend more time taking away others' suffering.

- While you are eating, walking, and at other times, think, "I am experiencing this depression on behalf of all sentient beings." Think that it is not *your* depression.

Enjoy your depression by voluntarily taking on the experience for all sentient beings and giving it to your ego, thus destroying it completely.

Enjoy your depression by voluntarily taking on the experience for all sentient beings and giving it to your ego, thus destroying it completely.

Think of your depression as the purification of past negative karma. If we don't experience it now, we will have to experience the hell realms for many years, so it is good to have it now.

- Think: "I am experiencing past heavy negative karma. By experiencing this I am purifying it."

In this way, you use your depression to achieve happiness, like transforming snake venom into medicine.

You can also use your depression to collect merit. Your depression becomes like performing the *preliminary practices* for purifying and collecting merit, such as making *mandala offerings* and hundreds of thousands of prostrations. It is like reciting the mantras of powerful deities. You use your depression to achieve not just worldly happiness but ultimate happiness.

Transform depression into the path to enlightenment and use it to develop compassion and bodhichitta for other sentient beings. This allows you to free sentient beings from their suffering more quickly and bring them to enlightenment.

Enjoy your depression by thinking of all these benefits.

With much love and prayers,

REMEMBER

- I am experiencing this depression on behalf of all sentient beings.
- This is not *my* depression.

Depression Is a Sign of Purification

Dear Lama Zopa,

I have been battling severe depression for some time. The depression often discourages me from doing my Dharma practice. What makes it even more difficult is that when I do practice, the depression sometimes feels worse before it gets better, when it gets better at all. (It does get better sometimes, and then I get excited, only to feel down when the depression returns.) I end up having strong doubts about whether meditation can bring the end of suffering. I hear stories of great practitioners who were able to transform tremendous difficulties and problems into happiness, but I have no idea whether a regular person like me could ever achieve that.

Rinpoche, is it really possible for someone like me to use depression to wake up and be happy?

Best wishes,
Juan, Mexico City

Transform depression into the path to enlightenment and use it to develop compassion and bodhichitta for other sentient beings.

DEPRESSION

The syllable Ah

When you wash a cloth with water and soap, the dirt comes out. It is the same when we practice Dharma: negative karma comes out very quickly.

Dear Juan,
The first thing is to

- ➤ Think: "Having depression is good. It is good because it is a sign of purification, of having practiced Dharma."

Negative karma gets purified at different levels.

1. At the first level, you never experience the suffering that would normally result from your actions.

2. At the second level, you experience the results, but rather than eons of suffering in the lower realms, the result manifests in this life as some smaller problem, such as a toothache or headache, or being criticized by people.

Unbelievably negative karma manifests in these ways, or even just as bad dreams, sickness, failure in business, a disaster in your family or in your relationships, other people treating you badly, abusing you, and also in the form of depression. This way, you never have to experience heavy suffering in other realms for an incredible length of time.

3. The next level of purifying karma is when you are reborn in the lower realms for a very short time and the suffering is very light.

Therefore, experiencing depression can be a positive thing. This way of thinking can be related to whatever problems you have so that you feel positive and happy about them. You should understand all of your problems in this way.

- ➤ Think: "How good to have depression!" This gives you inner strength.

When you throw a stone at a rock, for example, it hits it in one second, like a snap of your fingers. Similarly, in this way, all your heavy suffering is finished in one instant. This is very positive. It's fantastic! There is no question that the problems experienced in the human realm are an incredibly great comfort, even a pleasure, when you compare them to the extremely heavy sufferings in the hell, hungry ghost, and animal realms. You can relate this to AIDS, cancer, or whatever problems you have.

When you wash a cloth with water and soap, the dirt comes out. At first, the dirt is very black. This is a good sign. You want the cloth to be clean, so the dirt must come out. It is the same when we practice Dharma. At that time, negative karmas manifest and we can get sick. When we practice Dharma, negative karma comes out very quickly.

Having depression is like that; therefore, we should rejoice in depression. The karma is made to manifest and is finished by the depression or another problem. The soap and water is your Dharma practice. That is why many Dharma practitioners encounter a lot of obstacles when they perform powerful practice.

Those who don't perform any practice or purification—even someone who kills many thousands of beings every day—may have a very healthy body and live for many years. However, this is not a good sign. All their negative karma is stored up to be experienced in the future for an incredible length of time. Even when it is not experienced in the lower realms, it will manifest in the human realm for thousands of lifetimes. This life is very short. It's like one second. If you compare it with all our future lives or with the length of even one lifetime in the hell realms, it's nothing.

In *Guru Puja* by Panchen Lama Chokyi Gyaltsen, it says, "Should even the environment and the beings therein be filled with the fruit of our karmic debts, and unwished-for suffering pour down on us like rain, we seek your blessing to take those miserable conditions as a path by seeing them as causes to exhaust our negative karma."

> ☙ Think: "If everything in my life is unpleasant, the place where I live is ugly, and everybody gets angry at me, dislikes me, criticizes me, even harms me, I should look at these experiences as the cause that brings to an end the results of past heavy negative karma collected from beginningless rebirths."

In this way, you turn bad circumstances into positive ones. This way you always stay happy. This is the correct way of thinking, the way of Buddhist psychology.

You can understand why it is important to always keep the mind happy and why this is emphasized in the teachings. If the mind is unhappy, this also makes your family and other people around you unhappy. You are so caught up with yourself that your mind is not open to others. You cannot love others, help them, or make them happy. You cannot even smile at others, cannot give them even that small pleasure.

When you enjoy your life and your mind is happy, you have so much space in your mind to think of others, to cherish and love them. You have room to help others and feel compassion toward them. You can even give some pleasure to others by smiling. You are more relaxed, and you can do your job better.

Somebody who is practicing Dharma is able to continue doing his

When you enjoy your life and your mind is happy, you have so much space in your mind to think of others, to cherish and love them.

or her meditation practices, commitments, and prayers. Otherwise, if your mind is not happy due to depression, you may even stop practicing. You cannot recite even one *Om mani padme hum* mantra. When life is miserable, it is important to keep your mind happy by utilizing the path to enlightenment and thinking in this way. This is one example of thought transformation.

Every morning, when you begin the day, make a strong determination in your mind.

> • Think: "Whatever problem I encounter today, I won't allow my mind to be disturbed by it. I'm not going to allow myself to be weak. I'm going to challenge my problems. I am going to be strong."

Make a determination to transform your problems into happiness.

> • Think: "Even though the continuation of my mind has no beginning, what has prevented me from achieving enlightenment up until now is ego."

> • Think: "I have not achieved even the confidence that, if death comes, I will definitely have a good rebirth. Because I allow myself to be under the control of self-cherishing thoughts, I don't have even that confidence."

It is the ego that never gives us freedom to practice Dharma, brings us no peace or happiness, always disturbs us, and doesn't allow us to liberate others from the lower realms and from samsara. It also doesn't allow others to help us. What makes me harm others and others harm me is ego. Any undesirable thing that happens in my life is caused by ego: criticism from others, a bad reputation, abuse, and friends becoming enemies. Those who are harmonious with me become disharmonious because of my ego. Even though I know Dharma, I am unable to practice, meditate, or recite mantras or *sadhanas*. What prevents this is ego. Ego doesn't allow me to listen, reflect, meditate on Dharma, or do retreat. When we find time only for meaningless actions, it is ego's fault.

The meditation for depression is to destroy the ego. You visualize giving your depression to your ego by thinking,

> • Think: "Let my ego have the depression. Why do I need to experience it? Let it have my depression."

This way, you use your depression as the best healing—to heal the chronic disease of the self-cherishing thought, the continuation of which is beginningless. Depression becomes unbelievably useful, especially for

When we find time only for meaningless actions, it is ego's fault.

The Medicine Buddhas

having realizations of bodhichitta. It helps us get rid of our defilements and complete our realizations. Depression becomes extremely precious.

With much love and prayers,

REMEMBER

- I can utilize my bad experiences on the path. I can turn bad circumstances into positive ones.
- When I can keep my mind happy, there is so much space for others.
- What makes me harm others and others harm me is my ego.
- Depression is like dirt coming out in the wash, so I must rejoice.

Depression becomes unbelievably useful, especially for having realizations of bodhichitta.

71

Down Syndrome Baby

Dear Lama Zopa,

I am expecting a child and the doctors have given me the news that the baby may very likely have Down Syndrome, which may cause a severe mental disability. I just don't know what to think. My husband and I are in a state of shock. Is it best to have the baby? Is it possible for the baby to change in the womb? Please advise us, Rinpoche.

With much love,
Sally, Auckland

My very dear Sally,

Thank you very much for your kind email.

According to my divinations, there is a possibility that the baby may die in the womb, so you have to start practicing now. What comes out best is for you to perform strong Chenrezig practice and to recite the medium-length mantra.

1. **Visualize Chenrezig clearly on your crown and nectar coming from Chenrezig's heart or from his 1,000 arms and entering your body and, especially, the child's body and mind, purifying its imperfect organs and senses.**

2. **Visualize: the negative karma and obscurations come out of the child's body in the form of dirty water; the sicknesses come out in the form of pus and blood; and the harm from spirits comes out in the form of snakes, frogs, and scorpions. Mainly concentrate on the negative karma being purified.**

3. **Think: "My child is completely purified of all negative karma, defilements, spirit harm, and sicknesses.**

4. **Then visualize beams of light coming from Chenrezig and going out to the six realms, purifying all beings completely.**

Whether your child lives or dies, purification is the most important thing to improve its life, so it can have a perfect human body, practice Dharma, and achieve liberation and enlightenment by actualizing the path.

This is the most significant thing, and it can happen now while the child is in the womb. The negative karma can be purified; the child's body can change and not have this disability.

Perform very strong prayers and meditate on purifying the child's negative karma so it doesn't have to suffer, particularly in this life, by changing its karma.

The mantra of the Compassion Buddha, Om Mani Padme Hum

Perform very strong prayers and meditate on purifying the child's negative karma so it doesn't have to suffer, particularly in this life, by changing its karma.

- ☙ **Please, whatever you do, do it with a good heart to help others.**

With much love and prayers,

REMEMBER

....

- • **Whatever I do, I must do it with a good heart.** ....

Whether your child lives or dies, purification is the most important thing to improve its life.

Born Blind

Dear Lama Zopa,

We are writing to you hoping you can advise us. We will take your words into our hearts. My wife recently had a child, a little girl, who was born blind and with some physical deformities. Our little girl is now about three months old. At first, when she was born, we thought she might get better, maybe even recover her vision, but now this doesn't seem like it's going to happen.

We are very distressed. The situation seems so difficult, and even unfair, although I know this is a childish way of looking at things. But still, I can't help getting angry and desperate when I think about the future. Will she be like this forever? Of course we want to love and help our baby, so we are really trying to accept the situation. The difficult thing is knowing how to accept it, how to relate to it.

Why did this happen? How should we think about this situation in order to come to terms with it? Any advice you can give us will help us so much.

Love,
Gilles and Yvette, Toulouse

My very dear Gilles and Yvette,

Both of you should think of the situation many other children are in—many have great difficulties, such as being born as conjoined twins or deformed in other serious ways. Many families have to experience more difficult situations than yours. My point is you should not think you are the only ones in this situation. Take some time and contemplate that many other parents are in more difficult situations.

I am going to try to help you to know how to think about and relate to your situation. You should be very grateful to Buddha/God.

- Think: "Buddha/God gave us this small child to look after and to help us develop our spiritual practice, to purify heavy negative karma that we have created in the past."

- Think: "This is Buddha's gift, helping us to be free from our oceans of negative karmas, and this is Buddha's gift for me to develop my practice and to develop full enlightenment and peerless happiness."

You should not think you are the only ones in this situation. Take some time and contemplate that many other parents are in more difficult situations.

- Think: "Our child is cherished by countless buddhas and bodhisattvas—holy beings."

So many bodhisattvas collect vast amounts of merit every second and actualize the path for the benefit of every single being, including your child. So many buddhas completed the two types of merit and actualized the two *kayas* (two buddha bodies) for the benefit of all beings, including your child. There are so many buddhas and bodhisattvas, including Guru Shakyamuni Buddha, who sacrificed his life for three countless great eons, and gave up his family and wealth when he was a king; the whole point was to actualize the two types of merit for all sentient beings, which includes your child. Like that, there are so many buddhas, and all of them achieved enlightenment to benefit all sentient beings, which includes your child.

- Therefore, every day when you offer service to your child, this is the best offering to all the buddhas and bodhisattvas; this is the best puja for all the buddhas. You both should offer service to your child with this awareness and on the basis of this.

- Think: "Our child makes our life so meaningful, gives us a lot of satisfaction, and makes our life so fulfilling."

In your heart you should have the wish to benefit all sentient beings, to be able to enlighten countless sentient beings from samsaric suffering and bring them to full enlightenment.

- Of course, this doesn't mean you should not try different treatments for your child, I am not saying that.

There are many different methods to try to heal her: traditional and alternative, and there are many different kinds of healers, not just in hospitals. So, in the meantime, you can look for different methods, see if there is anything that can help her. This way you can feel that you have tried everything.

- I am very happy to hear that you both are thinking of accepting the situation; that is very important, because your child was born to you in this life, in this way, due to past karma, both your karma and the child's karma.

Negative karma is not inherently existent but is formed by wrong actions created by the mind in past lives; usually they are performed without your knowing the result that you are creating. Maybe the action was performed to try to achieve happiness at that time, but it was performed with a selfish mind, a mind of ignorance, attachment, and anger. Because

Of course, this doesn't mean you should not try different treatments for your child. There are many different methods to try to heal her: traditional and alternative, and there are many different kinds of healers, not just in hospitals.

of this attitude it became a negative karma and the result was suffering, maybe to be born like this.

> ✒ So, your child being born to you comes from karma on both sides. But this karma is not forever, it doesn't last long, it is a very temporary situation. You shouldn't think it is forever, because when death comes, one's life is like a dream, it's gone; all your plans for the future are gone.

It is good to remember this now because it helps you realize that this current situation, this life, having this child, could end at any minute.

This is a very broad way of thinking, a positive way of thinking. Your child, by showing this aspect, by being born like this, is also a teaching for you. If we don't practice Dharma and abandon negative karma, then we all can be born like this in the future. Your child is telling all of us that.

With much love and prayers,

REMEMBER

- Karma is not forever; it is temporary.
- Our child is a gift and is teaching us.
- We must abandon negative karma; otherwise we could be born like this in the future.

I am very happy to hear that you are both thinking of accepting the situation; that is very important, because your child was born to you in this life, in this way, due to past karma, both your karma and the child's karma.

Bush Fires

Dear Lama Zopa,
You have probably heard in the news about these bush fires that have
been burning out of control in Australia. Please, could you give us some
suggestions for what we at the Dharma centers can do to help pacify these
fires?

Love,
Wendy, Brisbane

Dear Wendy,
While the bush fires are still burning, the Australian Dharma centers
should

➤ **Perform a total of eleven Medicine Buddha *pujas*.**

If these pujas are done with strong prayers to Medicine Buddha
to stop the winds and to bring rain, this can definitely help the situation,
especially if the lamas at the centers also attend the pujas. According to
my divinations, Medicine Buddha puja would be very beneficial.

Love and prayers,

How to Help When There Are Natural Disasters?

····· *After a student who lived in an area prone to annual hurricanes*
sought his advice, Rinpoche wrote a general letter to his students,
recommending certain practices.

My dear loving compassionate readers,
You may wonder what to do, what prayers to make, when there are
disasters such as tornados, hurricanes, heavy rain, storms, floods,
earthquakes, or fires, as well as disasters that destroy crops and entire
towns and cities within one hour; disasters that cause so many billions of
dollars of damage, where so much money is spent to rebuild the towns;
disasters where many hundreds and thousands of people die or become
homeless, have no food or clean water, and so forth.

If these pujas
are done with
strong prayers to
Medicine Buddha
to stop the winds
and to bring the
rain, this can
definitely help.

Even though these kinds of problems are big, and even though there are countless buddhas,

- **If someone with a very sincere heart takes refuge one-pointedly, without any doubts, in even one buddha and recites that buddha's mantras, including the name mantra, this can change the situation completely.**

It can change natural disasters and prevent war. Whatever problems there are can be made less, and even completely stopped, if someone takes strong refuge and prays to even just one buddha. The weather can change in that very hour or in the next hour, by the power of one person making prayers.

There is no question that if the person who makes the prayers actually has realizations, then every single prayer, every single word, has incredible power; realizations such as

1. **Bodhichitta,**

2. **Emptiness,**

3. **Having a very pure heart, unstained by the *eight worldly concerns*, or**

4. **Living a pure life, in pure morality, by taking the vows of a layperson or an ordained person (a nun or a monk), but especially ordained.**

There are examples in Christianity as well as in Buddhism of bodhisattvas and great saints who were able to prevent flooding, completely change the direction of rivers, stop rivers altogether, and walk right across them to the other side.

When someone with any of these realizations prays, then the devas, *nagas,* and all the other beings, including the eight groups of worldly beings (who are very connected with the weather and the elements and who cause the elements to be destructive), will listen more and obey these practitioners. They will obey this person, and the harm and destruction from the elements can be stopped.

- **You can pray to many of the buddhas, such as *White Umbrella Deity*.**

She is very powerful for protecting from the danger of the elements. With strong faith and strong refuge, you can put her mantra or picture around your house. Then, visualize that rainfalls of nectar are emitted from the mantra. This nectar can stop fires, purify the suffering of insects, and purify the negative karma of all sentient beings. All are liberated.

- **Recite prayers to buddhas such as *Lion-Face Dakini*, Chenrezig, or *Padmasambhava*.**

Visualize them and then recite the mantra with full confidence. Rely upon them, thinking that they have all the power and have manifested for us, sentient beings, in different aspects for different purposes, for sentient beings who have that karma.

> ● **You can also do the practice of Medicine Buddha.**

This is not only meant for healing. It is also very powerful for achieving success and for solving problems; for someone who has died, for family problems, for someone who is sick, for attaining happiness and freedom from suffering, for finding a job, for success in business, and so on.

There are examples in Christianity as well as in Buddhism of bodhisattvas and great saints who were able to prevent flooding, completely change the direction of rivers, stop rivers altogether, and walk right across them to the other side.

There is one story of Lama Kelsang Jamyang Monlam, who had bodhichitta realizations. When Tashi Lhunpo monastery was in danger of being flooded, he wrote on a stone, "If it is true that I have bodhichitta, then the water should turn back." After writing this on the stone, the river actually turned and went backward.

There is a story about the great St. Francis of Assisi. One time he was living and meditating in a cave with his disciples. His disciples asked St. Francis to stop the water that flowed inside the cave and that was disturbing their meditation. St. Francis went to the place where the water was flowing down the mountain and said, "Sister, my disciples can't meditate." Then the water stopped flowing from that time until the present day. It would be considered very inauspicious if the water started to flow again.

> ● **The water stopped flowing due to the power of St. Francis's bodhichitta.**

St. Francis's mind was totally pure; there was no stain of the eight worldly concerns, and he was totally renounced: a pure, spiritual person. You can feel his gentleness even from his statues and from his face, which is a sign of having bodhichitta and a totally tame, subdued mind. He seems so peaceful and humble and wonderful to look at, very inspirational. All the birds loved him and always stayed around him and on his body. This is also a sign that he was a great holy being, a saint.

One great Tibetan master who was a top scholar and a former abbot of Sera Je had a cat. Sera is one of the largest monastic universities around Lhasa, the capital of Tibet, where many thousands of monks

St. Francis went to the place where the water was flowing down the mountain and said, "Sister, my disciples can't meditate." Then the water stopped flowing from that time until the present day.

79

DISASTERS

study. From the moment the cat came to live with the abbot, it stopped catching and eating mice. Even when the cat saw mice running around the room, it just stayed very quietly near the abbot. This was due to the abbot's blessing, due to his tamed mind, his bodhichitta blessing, and his good heart.

> ◆ **The abbot's bodhichitta transformed even the cat's mind so that it did not harm others.**

Some years ago, it was reported in the news that a hurricane was going to hit Florida. A long-time student rang me to ask me to make prayers. I did some Mickey Mouse prayers,* and then I gave him the job of reciting the bodhisattva *Kshitigarbha's* mantra (even though he had asked me to do it). He made strong prayers by taking refuge in the bodhisattva Kshitigarbha. The hurricane didn't hit Florida but went around. He was so astonished that he rang me and said, "It worked!"

Even when there are problems in other places, other countries, you can definitely help by performing these practices with a sincere heart, full of faith. Even if we ourselves are not in danger, we have the responsibility to protect other sentient beings.

REMEMBER

- With faith, praying to even one buddha can help change disasters.
- Even when there are problems in other places, other countries, I can definitely help by performing these practices with a sincere heart, full of faith.

Even if we ourselves are not in danger, we have the responsibility to protect other sentient beings.

* Lama Zopa doesn't pray to Mickey Mouse; he is simply expressing humility.

80

A Failed Operation

Dear Lama Zopa,
About a year ago, I had a car accident and decided to have plastic surgery on my face. To make a long story short, there were complications, and the operation left me disfigured. I have been struggling with depression ever since. To make everything worse, my boyfriend of many years has decided to break up with me because he is embarrassed by my disfigurement and says he doesn't love me anymore.

I have spent a lot of time thinking about what to do with my life now. I am trying to put into practice the teachings in your book, Transforming Problems into Happiness, *and want to use what has happened to me to be of benefit to others. I am considering going to work at the Maitri Leprosy Centre in Bodhgaya, India, because I feel that I can understand what those people must be feeling.*

Rinpoche, please tell me whether this is a good idea.
Best wishes,
Josefina, Madrid

Dear Josefina,

- It would be incredibly good to go and work at the leprosy center. I put my two thumbs up! It's the best thing to do.

Don't think about your face. Offering service will give you so much peace and joy in your heart. Also, because you will be busy there, it will take your mind off of your face and your boyfriend, which have tortured you so much.

Also,

- You can help with the *Universal Education school* project in Bodhgaya, and

- You can meditate on how to practice kindness to others.

Love and many prayers,

Don't think about your face. Offering service will give you so much peace and joy in your heart.

Remember Loving Kindness

Dear Lama Zopa,
I had a very painful childhood, and as a result I have a lot of trouble
trusting others. I am trying to let go of blame for my parents and
circumstances and to understand that my situation now is my own karma,
but I still have a hard time trusting anyone. I don't know whether this is
some type of attachment; it feels so reasonable, given my experience.
Thank you for taking the time to think about my problem.

Love,
June, Wisconsin

Dear June,

- **Practice loving kindness meditation so that your**
  compassion will grow.

Understand other beings' suffering. The main thing to remember is
loving kindness.

With much love and prayers,

What is better then
boddhicita in this life
I am filled up with
bliss. over the hairs.

Understand other
beings' suffering.

If Divorce Happens, Let It Happen

Dear Lama Zopa,
I am going through a terrible time right now. My wife wants a divorce after several years of marriage. I've tried hard in this relationship, but it seems like there was nothing I could do to satisfy her, and we've both been miserable for some time. But now that she wants to end the marriage, I feel like a terrible failure. Isn't divorce wrong? Is there anything I can do to save the marriage?

Best wishes for your health,
Charlie, Copenhagen

Dear Charlie,
If divorce happens, let it happen. Don't be too upset. Divorce means that you are experiencing negative karma from a past life, such as from sexual misconduct with someone else's partner, or sex at the wrong time or place. Divorce can also be the result of the karmas of slander, creating disunity, and causing others to split up. Therefore,

> ● Think: "She is now leaving me, so the bad karma I created to experience this result is finishing; it is being purified."

If you look at the situation in a positive way, it becomes like poison leaving your system. This brings peace of mind.

> ● Think: "Whatever is best in my life must be dedicated to the benefit of sentient beings. Whatever I experience—praise, criticism, even being reborn in the hell realms—may it be most beneficial for all sentient beings, for them to achieve enlightenment as quickly as possible."

This is the best psychology to practice.

Your only real job is to work for sentient beings, to bring them to enlightenment. When you think like this, you can use your problem like a medicine to relieve suffering and bring about happiness. A peacock thrives on eating poisonous plants; for others they are just poison. By using your painful experience as a means to experience all other living beings' problems, you are making it the best medicine and the best way to achieve enlightenment.

We suffer so much in relationships, with anger and jealousy, but we can use these to generate compassion. Your wife is teaching you

If you look at the situation in a positive way, it becomes like poison leaving your system.

83

renunciation from samsara and attachment; she is showing you freedom by helping you learn to cut your attachment.

When you let go of your attachment, you will find satisfaction.

REMEMBER

- My only real job is to work for others.
- My wife is showing me how to cut attachment.

Should I Divorce?

Dear Rinpoche,
I am thinking seriously of divorcing my husband. We don't really get along that well, and he doesn't seem to understand my Dharma practice. We have been married many years, and there just doesn't seem to be any life to the marriage. Still, I don't want to hurt him as I don't think he would take it very well. He would feel we have invested too much time into our marriage to separate.

What will be the karmic results if I ask for a divorce? My husband is only one person, but still, I have been close to him for many years, and I do have unique responsibilities as his wife. What should I do, Rinpoche?

Love,
Amanda, Portland

Dear Amanda,
Divorce is just another action.

- ➥ **Like eating, walking, sitting, or sleeping, whether the action is negative or positive depends on the motivation.**

When you are making a life decision, it is much clearer if you analyze on the basis of the goal of benefiting others. Then, if it is beneficial, you do it. If it's not beneficial, then don't. If you don't have a clear goal for the action, then it is very confusing trying to decide.

When you let go of your attachment, you will find satisfaction.

84

Generally, there are only two goals to consider when making a decision:

- Either it is for one's own happiness or for the happiness of others.

Why do we have to think of benefiting others? Because the purpose of our life is to be useful to others, to free all other beings from all suffering. Therefore, the decision has to be made on that basis.

- Think: "Other beings are so kind."

Even to produce one grain of rice, people have to plant seedlings in a field then move them to another field to grow. They have to water the plants. When the land is being fertilized, so many ants and other beings are killed. So much negative karma is created just to produce rice. Since so many sentient beings suffered just for one grain of rice, there is no way you can eat a grain of rice thinking only of your own happiness. So many sentient beings suffered to make an entire plate of rice. There are also many sentient beings living in the vegetables and the water. So many sentient beings suffer so we can enjoy our meal.

- Think: "Each day, each hour, it is only through the kindness of others that we survive."

So, we must do something for others. We can't just abandon them.

Love and prayers,

REMEMBER

- Whether an action is good or not depends on my motivation.
- The purpose of my life is to benefit others.

It's Better for You to Divorce

Dear Lama Zopa,
I am having difficulties with my marriage. My husband and I do not get along at all any more. We fight constantly. His very presence fills me with anger, and vice-versa. We try to stay away from each other, and when we are together, we barely speak in order to avoid fighting. I see nothing good

We must do something for others. We can't just abandon them.

in our relationship anymore. In fact, being together seems to be harmful: maintaining a virtuous mind in his presence is not possible for me, and I think it's the same with him. I have suggested a divorce, but he hasn't said anything.

Please, what do you think? Do you think we should try to work things out and stay together, or would it be more beneficial for us to divorce?

> *Best wishes,*
> *Sevtap, Istanbul*

Dear Sevtap,

Although I more often counsel married couples to keep trying to work things out, in this case,

> ☙ **I advise you that it would be more beneficial for you both to separate and meet other partners.**

Although you don't have the karma for your relationship to be beneficial, the fact that you are together indicates that you have some previous karma to deal with. You are now married to a person who was created by your delusions and karma. So, you are married to the result of your own delusion and karma.

The solution is to change the circumstances so that the relationship ends harmoniously. For this, I suggest that you

> ☙ **Make prayers for your husband to find another woman to whom he is attracted, and who would benefit his mind.**

This way he will leave you with a happy mind, and the separation will be harmonious. If the prayers are made with the motivation for the most beneficial outcome, then there will naturally be more power to the prayers.

For this, you have to purify your previous karma with your husband and make prayers for him to find a suitable partner. Until the karma is purified, there will be difficulties to experience.

With much love and prayers,

The solution is to change the circumstances so that the relationship ends harmoniously.

REMEMBER

- **Generate the motivation for the most beneficial outcome.**
- **Until the karma is purified, there will be difficulties.**

Dear Lama Zopa,

My name is Emily, and I am almost eighty years old. I have had a full life and am starting to think about my death. I deeply appreciate the Buddhist teachings about being of benefit to others, so it occurred to me to donate my organs after I die. I am not sure that they would even take them because I am so old, but I would like to try.

I am also concerned about how to die peacefully and what instructions I should give to my family members about how I would like to pass away. I have heard about a certain Tibetan Buddhist practice that helps the consciousness leave the body in the most peaceful way, but I don't know anything about it and am afraid if I don't talk to my children soon, they won't know what to do. Can you please give me some advice about this? Thank you so very much.

Love,
Emily, Sydney

Dear Emily,
It is excellent that you have the intention of giving your body to others.

Normally, in Tibet, where it is cold and dry, you can keep a body for three days without any problems. If the body starts to smell immediately, it means the consciousness has left the body, and you don't need to keep the body after that.

In the West, if a person dies at home, there's more opportunity to let some time pass before you take out the organs. This is important because you need to wait until the consciousness has left the body before you touch it. However, I think, even in the hospital, if somebody discussed the situation with the doctor, maybe they could wait for ten minutes, fifteen minutes, half an hour, or an hour. It's good not to take the organs immediately, right after the breath has stopped. You need time for the consciousness to leave the body.

The important thing is when the breath has stopped. At that time, the body is still soft. It is the same as if you were sleeping. You can tell your family the following:

1. **Don't touch any part of your body during this time. Just leave it.**

2. **Wait for whatever period of time the doctor says they can wait.**

Try to to wait until the consciousness has left the body before you touch it…It's good not to take the organs immediately, right after the breath has stopped.

87

3. Just before that amount of time has passed, without touching any other part of the body, touch the crown of your head; pull the hair on the crown strongly.

4. If you have a special *powa pill*, they can put it on your crown.

5. If you are still in a state of meditation after the breath has stopped, then when it is time to move your body for the organ transplant, your family can light incense; this helps you stop your meditation.

6. Then your consciousness leaves your body.

7. Now it is fine to move your body and donate the organs.

If your consciousness leaves through the crown, it goes to the *formless realms* or to the pure land of Buddha. There are only these two ways. At that time, all bad karma becomes good karma.

Actually, you can tell your family to put the powa pill on the crown when the breath is just about to stop. (You can ask the lama at your Buddhist center for one of these pills.)

Love and prayers,

It is excellent that you have the intention of giving your body to others.

REMEMBER

• It's important that your body is not touched for as long as possible after you have stopped breathing.

Recognizing Dreams As Dreams

Dear Lama Zopa,
I had a dream where I saw myself as a monk together with other monks
trapped as prisoners. I realized I could escape but was instead thrown in a
lake where maybe I died. I have had the dream many times and wanted to
know if it was a memory of a past life and also how the dream can benefit
others.

Love,
Cara, Granada

My dear Cara,
Thank you for your letter. At the moment we have not achieved
liberation from samsara and have not reached enlightenment. We are
circling around in samsara since time without beginning, even if we have
been monks in many past lives. The most important thing to do is to
train the mind every day, and you can even do this in your dreams (as
we are continually dreaming).

This may seem simple, but in fact it is very profound:

- **When you are dreaming, recognize it as a dream. If
  you can remember during your dream that you are
  dreaming, then you can use that time to perform
  virtuous actions, like practicing Dharma.**

Whatever situation comes up in your dreams, you can work with it. This
is very intelligent.

- **If you recognize your dreams as dreams, then if
  someone hurts you in the dream, you can overcome it.**

- **If in your dreams you see something very beautiful, you
  can work with attachment.**

Ignorance makes us see things as truly existent. If you can see
them as a dream, as a false dream, recognize dreams as dreams, then
you can practice profound meditation that acts as an antidote to wrong
conceptions.

- **When you are not dreaming, not asleep, you can see
  also that as a dream.**

This can help you see that external objects that appear as if they were
not merely labeled by the mind, but appear as real, as existing from their
own side, are untrue. This means that in your heart you can understand
that they are empty, that they don't exist from their own side.

*The most
important thing to
do is to train the
mind every day,
and you can even
do this in your
dreams.*

DREAMS

This is a very effective meditation because you go directly to the base of the ignorance. This will help you actualize negation of the objects of ignorance, because you realize that they don't exist from their own side. There is not even one atom that appears from its own side, not one particle of any object or action; you see all of it as empty. You overcome the ignorance that creates delusions, which in turn create more delusions that lead to negative thoughts and then to the creation of karma. It is this that produces the ocean of samsara. This is why we should look for total liberation from the ocean of suffering.

The root of the delusions is ignorance. By means of your wisdom that realizes emptiness, it is possible to liberate yourself and to reach enlightenment and develop wisdom and bodhichitta.

> If you have received a *highest yoga tantra initiation* you can perform the practices of the *Six Yogas of Naropa* and other *dream yogas,* and you can realize these practices.

Also, with correct devotion to the guru, you can realize all the stages of the path. Correct devotion to the guru is the root of all realizations.

You should feel very fortunate to practice Dharma, and if you know *tantra* you should put it into practice.

This is my advice to you.

With much love and prayers,

This can help you see that external objects that appear as if they were not merely labeled by the mind, but appear as real, as existing from their own side, are untrue.

REMEMBER

- **Seeing my dreams as dreams is a very effective meditation because I go directly to the base of ignorance.**

Defeating the Enemy

Dear Lama Zopa,

I am concerned for my daughter's life because she has been addicted to drugs off and on for many years. She started when her father died. I think she just couldn't face the loss. I am her only moral support now and I want to help her, but I just don't know what to do. She has too many friends who do drugs, and her whole lifestyle has been centered around the drug culture. I can see her predicament, and I can understand why it is hard for her to give up her drug life even though she has temporarily overcome her physical addiction a number of times. Is there anything I can do to help her?

Love,

Michelle, North Carolina

Dear Michelle,

As far as the drugs are concerned, I did a divination and it came out very good for your daughter

- **To go to *Kopan Monastery* in Nepal and do a meditation course.**

In order to benefit her mind,

- **She should look inside herself to gain knowledge to improve her quality of life.**

This will inspire her to give some meaning to her life. She needs an environment with people who protect her, who are not involved with these things.

- **She should stay away from people who are connected with drugs and not make friends with them.**

She can give compassion and love to them but not physical friendship. Physically, she should keep away. That also helps protect her from contracting HIV.

- **She should make a really strong determination from her heart to challenge her attachment to taking drugs, to seeking that pleasure. She should determine to overcome it as if she were going to war, trying to defeat her enemy.**

It's like in a boxing match, where you try to defeat your opponent, but here you defeat your own thoughts, the desire that brings your life down, making it meaningless and sick, causing you to destroy your life through this attachment to the pleasure of drugs.

It's like in a boxing match, where you try to defeat your opponent, but here you defeat your own thoughts, the desire that brings your life down, making it meaningless and sick, causing you to destroy your life through this attachment to the pleasure of drugs.

The best friends to protect her in this way are the sangha.

  ☙ **For her to be with nuns is best, though it could also be lay women.**

At the very least they should be people who are not taking drugs, preferably people who have a strong practice, strong discipline, and who are living a pure life. If she is with those kinds of friends, she will be protected by them.

This kind of problem takes a long time to resolve. It will not be resolved in just one month.

  ☙ **She needs to stay in a place where she cannot find drugs for a long time. That would be the best thing, until she has made a strong determination from her heart to abandon drugs, feeling totally disgusted with them, and until she wants to help herself and others.**

If she wants to live with a man, she can do that. But since she wants to have a long and healthy life, she should be careful. If she decides to live with a man, she should examine and check the person well for a long time. The best would be a man who can protect her, who is good-hearted, with strong discipline and living a pure life. It would also be best for him to be practicing Buddhism, especially Mahayana Buddhism. It would be good if she can get support from him in this way.

Generally, since she is a woman, I think it is best for her to be with nuns or lay women who have the qualities that I mentioned.

  ☙ **Maybe it would be good to tell her that her life can give so much happiness to others: She can give the happiness of this life, the happiness of future lives, and the highest happiness, enlightenment, to countless other beings.**

There are so many incredible, wonderful, beautiful things you can do for others and also, of course, for yourself.

Instead, we completely destroy this. We make our lives completely meaningless by following desire and self-cherishing, thinking of *my* happiness, *my* pleasure. By being attached to just this life and sensual pleasures, we stop the development of our mind. We prevent ourselves from realizing the ultimate nature of our own mind: the buddha potential, or *buddha nature*. This stops us from seeing the good part of ourselves and blocks us from developing our minds. It blocks our path to enlightenment, our spiritual path. It is not easy because we have so much habitual behavior from the past.

There are so many incredible, wonderful, beautiful things you can do for others and also, of course, for yourself.

So, this problem requires two solutions.

1. The first is to study Dharma, to meditate and control the attachment through renunciation. This means giving freedom to herself, away from the enemy—the prison of attachment. This is not just to protect her from the problem of drugs; it helps bring happiness in future lives.

2. The second factor is the environment. The kind of people she is around is very important.

This is unbelievably important and is something that should be done right now, because death can come at any time. This is also the main cause for achieving everlasting happiness, total liberation from samsara and from all suffering. Benefiting others is the foundation for achieving enlightenment. The benefit from practicing meditation is not just that you stop taking drugs.

Drugs are just one example. There are many other habits that we can get addicted to, such as sexual misconduct, which bring us so many problems in life and block the development of our mind on the spiritual path. This happens if we don't continue to develop our mind on the spiritual path. Not only do we then continuously create problems, we always get stuck in them. It's like sinking in quicksand and never being able to get out our whole life. We then die in that quicksand. Our whole life finishes sadly, not achieving any satisfaction, happiness, or peace in our heart, not even for ourselves.

On top of this, we can't benefit others if we can't develop our mind on the spiritual path. When I say spiritual path, I mean developing the mind in renunciation, bodhichitta, and emptiness. On top of that, there is the tantric path. Besides not being able to offer deep benefit, we cannot offer even the small benefits that we can perform with our body, speech, and mind—just simple things in daily life—because our self-cherishing thoughts stop that. Ego doesn't allow us to do even that.

Because our minds are very weak, even if we know meditation techniques well or understand the teachings, just knowing them doesn't mean we can immediately apply them or that our mind immediately becomes strong. It takes time, and we might miss many opportunities to apply what we have learned. That is why having the protection of the right environment is very important. If we are with those kinds of people, our life can be protected by them.

- Later, when our mind is stabilized and strong, with total renunciation of these things, it doesn't matter. Even

Drugs are just one example. There are many other habits that we can get addicted to, such as sexual misconduct, which bring us so many problems in life and block the development of our mind on the spiritual path.

if we're living with people who are taking drugs, we won't have the slightest interest.

We won't engage in those things. It's the same after we have stable realizations of renunciation, bodhichitta, and wisdom. Then, even when we mix with people, working in an organization to serve others, our work doesn't become a cause of confusion to ourselves or to others. Our service and direction is very clear, so our work is not stained by attachment, anger, or ego. If the mind is holy, it becomes only holy work, holy service. There is no danger for us and no danger for others. We are free from the problems that many people commonly experience when they live with people and work for others.

If we live with good friends of the kind I mentioned—strong Dharma practitioners with some discipline, who protect karma, do a lot of practice, understand Dharma, and live a pure life—we become like those friends and lead a better life. If we have bad friends, we become like them, too. That is because as ordinary beings, we do not have control over our minds or stable realizations and are under the power of our environment. When we don't meditate on lamrim in our daily lives, we are controlled by the environment, by the people around us, and so forth. We are controlled by our own hallucinations, even when we are alone.

When we don't meditate, impermanent phenomena appear as permanent, and we believe in that; dependent things appear as independent and inherently existent, and we believe in that. That is how we get overwhelmed by external things, by our own hallucinations. Therefore, the right environment is a very important protection for our life.

With much love and prayers,

By being attached to just this life and sensual pleasures, we stop the development of our mind. We prevent ourselves from realizing the ultimate nature of our own mind: the buddha potential, or buddha nature.

REMEMBER

- When we don't meditate, impermanent things appear as permanent, and we believe in that; dependent things appear as independent, and we believe in that.
- The right environment is very important.
- We make our lives meaningless by following self-cherishing.
- If we live with good friends we become like those friends and lead a better life.

Why Do Earthquakes Happen?

Dear Lama Zopa,

Here in Taiwan we have been experiencing a number of major earthquakes. The scientists tell us that Taiwan is located in a geologically unstable area and that we are close to some large fault lines. This is the reason they give for the earthquakes, and they give similar explanations based on natural causes for other disasters, such as floods, or hurricanes, and so forth.

I accept all that, and I can see that there have to be natural causes and conditions for these phenomena, but still, my question is: Why do they happen? Why do they happen now and not at some other time? Why do some people have these problems and not others? What are the real causes? If we know these causes, would it be possible to stop them from happening? Is there anything at all that we can do to prevent these disasters, or even smaller individual problems, like diseases? What is the best way to handle all these problems that come up in life?

Thank you for listening to my questions.

Love,

Joe, Taiwan

Dear Joe,

As far as what scientists say about earthquakes, they never mention the mind, the doer who experiences things. They explain what happens purely in terms of external evolution. Even if this is correct, it is only a short-term explanation. It doesn't really explain *why* these events happened in the first place.

From the simplest teachings of Buddhism, you can understand where hurricanes and earthquakes come from.

➤ They come as a result of past negative actions.

The cause of the karma to experience these things can be committing one or several of the ten nonvirtues. It could be the karmic result of

➤ Stealing,

➤ Ill will toward others, and

➤ Heresy

(for example, saying that reincarnation doesn't exist or that the Buddha, Dharma, and Sangha don't exist as objects of refuge). Part of the karmic result of heresy could be not having shelter or guidance after an

Any external explanation, even if it is correct, is just an explanation of the conditions for these problems. Without the inner cause—the negative karma—the outer condition for this problem couldn't occur.

earthquake. It could also be the karmic result of killing or of any of the other ten nonvirtues.

It is due to karma that we experience an earthquake or hurricane. The mind that has this experience comes as a result of self-cherishing thoughts, from either attachment or anger, which are closely related.

> ⤏ **The real root of these is ignorance, the unknowing mind, the mind that does not know the ultimate nature of mind, the "I," or other phenomena.**

There is the cause—karma—and then there are the conditions. The earthquake is not coming from outside; it is coming from your mind. We should also remember that even if outer precautions are taken, if there is a cause for harm, then that will be the result. For example, buildings that have been constructed with all the precautions against earthquakes have still been destroyed during earthquakes. Buildings constructed without any earthquake precautions have been left undamaged. If there is a cause for the building to be destroyed, it will happen. If not, it will not. This is according to the view of all four schools of Buddhist philosophy. They all accept what Shakyamuni Buddha said, "You are your own guide and also your own enemy."

This is reality. Every day, whether we have problems or happiness is due to what we do with our minds, how we make our minds think. If we make our mind think positively, we have peace. If we make our mind think negatively, we have problems.

Ultimately,

> ⤏ **The best solution would be not to experience these problems ever.**

> ⤏ **This is possible if, in our everyday life, we purify the causes of these problems,**

which are within us, not outside: our negative, disturbing, emotional thoughts, the self-centered mind.

In relation to this mind,

> ⤏ **Ignorance, anger, and attachment arise.**

> ⤏ **Then we engage in actions that become negative due to these negative attitudes and create the negative karma that harms others and ourselves.**

Any external explanation, even if it is correct, is just an explanation of the conditions for these problems. Without the inner cause—the negative karma—the outer condition for this problem couldn't occur.

- Every day, we should pray to purify our past negative karma and try to abstain from creating negative karma.

This is why it is important to take vows (as a layperson or monk or nun), to live in morality, and to not create negative karma.

- Taking vows, mentally making the decision to not do something, helps us not to commit negative karma again.

Even if you cannot take the vows in the presence of holy objects, the community of Sangha, or from your spiritual teacher, you can still strongly make the decision to abstain from negative karma and live in morality.

The conclusion is: the best, ultimate solution for problems is Dharma practice, especially actualizing the path within your own mind and purifying the causes—karma and delusion—of every suffering (rebirth, old age, sickness, and death).

This is also the best solution for all sicknesses and health problems, such as cancer, and is the best solution in order to live a long life, to be healthy, to have wealth, power, and a good reputation, to have harmony, to be peaceful and happy, to receive help from others, to receive affection and love from others, to receive support, and so forth.

Love and prayers,

REMEMBER

- Earthquakes are the result of past negative karma.
- What scientists say is just a relatively short-term explanation.
- The best solution for all sicknesses and to have a good life is to purify the causes of suffering and refrain from negativities.

Every day, whether we have problems or happiness is due to what we do with our minds, how we make our minds think. If we make our mind think positively, we have peace. If we make our mind think negatively, we have problems.

Bruised Ego

Dear Lama Zopa,

One of my colleagues, someone more senior than me, is constantly insulting me and my work. I feel like my ego is always bruised, and I am constantly annoyed and angry with this person. Needless to say, this situation is making me miserable and my performance is getting worse. Due to my family's financial situation, I can't afford to leave this job right now, so I have to find a way to deal with it.

I figure I should try to take on this situation as part of my Dharma practice, since I don't have a choice. How can I do this?

Love,
Tim, Texas

Dear Tim,

When our ego is harmed, we should rejoice. How wonderful it is!

In the same way as ordinary people react when their enemy is harmed or when some trouble happens to them, we should rejoice and feel so happy when our ego is hurt.

> ☙ Think: "How fantastic it is that my ego is harmed."

If you are practicing lamrim, thought transformation, and bodhichitta, then when something hurts your ego, you should

> ☙ Think: "This is exactly what I need. Let my ego have it and even greater harm."

The stronger the harm to our ego, the more quickly we destroy it. Treat your ego the way many Americans treat Osama bin Laden, who out of ignorance are pleased if he is harmed.

> ☙ Think: "My ego is trillions of times more harmful than Osama bin Laden."

Love and many prayers,

In the same way as ordinary people react when their enemy is harmed or when some trouble happens to them, we should rejoice and feel so happy when our ego is hurt.

REMEMBER

• I should be glad when my ego is hurt.

Ebola Outbreak

Dear Lama Zopa,

Here in Africa, we are experiencing a lot of concern and fear over a recent outbreak of Ebola. It is just one of many infectious diseases with the capacity to decimate huge populations, causing so much suffering and grief.

I have faith in karma and understand there are past causes. Is there something I can do as a practitioner to help prevent the immense amount of suffering caused by contagious disease?

Best wishes,
Patrick, Johannesburg

Dear Patrick,

The best practice to avert war and also diseases like Ebola is that of the female deity *Logyönma*. If people gather and perform a lot of Logyönma practice, this can prevent their spread.

One time in Dharamsala, India, there was a serious disease killing many people. Every day, for many months, the people in Dharamsala gathered together and did Logyönma practice. In this way, they were able to prevent the disease from taking over.

In fact, there are various practices that are good for Ebola and epidemic diseases:

1. **Logyönma,**

2. *Vajrapani Hayagriva Garuda,*

3. **Mantra Purifying All Negative Karma and Defilements,**

4. *The Exalted King of the Mantra of the Great Breath.*

People can also wear the latter mantra as protection.

Students can go to places where there is an epidemic and perform these practices. They can recite them and teach them to others in order to change the karma. When the people hear the students chanting the mantras, this can also help them.

With much love and prayers,

Logyönma

When the people hear the students chanting the mantras, this can also help them.

REMEMBER

- I can help change the karma of those who are suffering.

Removing Life Support

Dear Lama Zopa,
Our baby is terminally ill and is only kept alive by regular resuscitation
from cardiac/respiratory system arrests. The court has been asked to decide
whether the hospital should resuscitate him the next time it happens. We
simply do not know what is best to do. Please help us decide.

Much gratitude,
Bobby, Melbourne

Dear Bobby,
This decision completely depends on whether the child's next *rebirth*
would be in a lower or higher realm.

If the child will go on to greater suffering, then it is better to keep
him alive even for one hour. If the next rebirth will be in the god realm,
for instance, then it is okay to let him go.

So, how can we decide? I advised a student in such a situation

1. **To pray to Tara with great faith,**

2. **Then write every possible answer on pieces of paper,
   which you roll up very tightly, put in a bowl, and shake.**

3. **Choose one piece of paper and**

4. **Follow that advice.**

It is most important to have *every* alternative written down and
to have complete faith that whatever answer comes will be the right one.
This way you do not take on the karma of that decision.

As we are not able to make the decision ourselves we have to ask
for the help of a higher being.

Love and prayers,

If the child will
go on to greater
suffering, then it is
better to keep him
alive even for one
hour. If the next
rebirth will be in
the god realm, for
instance, then it is
okay to let him go.

REMEMBER

- **If I am not capable of making the decision myself,
  I must ask for the help of a higher being.**

Be Famous with Bodhichitta

Dear Lama Zopa,
Recently, some of my friends have been dying, one after another, and this led me to think about my own death and my inner life. It has caused me to study Dharma more intensively. I read in Pabongka Rinpoche's commentary on Lama Tsongkhapa's Three Principal Paths *that there are even* yogis *and great masters who cannot give up attachment to their famous reputation.*

I felt shocked. I had a moment of strong self-recognition. I saw how attached I myself was to my own reputation, how, even though my mind was very dedicated, I craved at a deep level to have good things said about me, to be thought well of, even to be famous.

My question is: How does one begin to lessen this attachment to one's good name and fame?

Best wishes,
Gilbert, Sydney

Dear Gilbert,
Of course, it takes a long time to change, to develop your mind. The correct way to do this is with the motivation of bodhichitta.

> ✤ **If you have realizations of bodhichitta—as well as emptiness and renunciation—then it is okay to be famous and have a reputation, because there is no danger for your mind. There is only great benefit.**

If you are a bodhisattva, even if others harm you, they receive benefit in return, in this life and in future lives, even by merely hearing your name. That is the special quality of a bodhisattva. He or she makes everything worthwhile. Even though those who harm a bodhisattva create negative karma on the one hand, on the other they have the advantage of meeting that bodhisattva again and again. That is because a bodhisattva prays only for good things to happen to sentient beings, including those who harm others or who harm the bodhisattva himself or herself.

It is like chemicals that you put in a huge water tank or reservoir to kill germs and make it drinkable. Although the amount of chemicals is small, it affects so much water drunk by many millions of people. By having realizations, especially bodhichitta, one person can benefit the world powerfully. It is so dynamic, such a benefit. Otherwise, having power, wealth, or a big reputation is only a condition for more suffering.

Look at the differences made by His Holiness the Dalai Lama, who brings unbelievable peace and happiness to millions of people in the world: benefits the size of the sky.

➤ **Without a Dharma mind, without the motivation of renunciation, bodhichitta, and emptiness, without living with a good heart—the thought of benefiting others— everything is suffering.**

It doesn't matter how famous you are or how many millions you have, it is all just suffering. It's nothing special.

More power and more fame mean more suffering and a greater danger of creating more negative karma. Not only is there suffering for you, but without a good heart, power becomes dangerous for others.

Power can be misused, and instead of bringing great benefit, can cause great harm. But with a good heart, even without the realization of bodhichitta, there is no danger of others receiving harm, only benefit.

Look at the differences made by His Holiness the Dalai Lama, who brings unbelievable peace and happiness to millions of people in the world: benefits the size of the sky. And then there is what Mao Tse-Tung did or what Hitler did. It is all a question of a person's mind, whether compassion is present or not.

➤ **Then you can think of the great Italian saint, St. Francis, and how much he benefited others. He totally renounced samsaric pleasures. He didn't like to be praised by others or by his students; he only liked criticism.**

Bodhisattvas sometimes decide to reincarnate in families of wealth and reputation so that they can offer charity to others. Also, bodhisattvas show, by their own example, that although they have everything, they see only suffering. Guru Shakyamuni Buddha renounced his power and wealth and went into retreat in solitary places after having seen the nature of samsara.

Love and prayers,

Bodhisattvas sometimes decide to reincarnate in families of wealth and reputation so that they can offer charity to others.

REMEMBER

- More power and more fame mean more suffering and a greater danger of creating more negative karma.
- Power can be misused, and instead of bringing great benefit, can cause great harm. But with a good heart, there is no danger of others receiving harm, only benefit.

Dear Lama Zopa,

I recently got a wonderful job that requires me to travel a lot. My problem is that ever since I was a child, I have been terrified of flying on planes. I really like this job and don't want my performance to be negatively affected, so I have tried different strategies to address the fear, like visualizing everything going fine and even hypnosis, but so far it hasn't worked. Do you have any suggestions for working with this fear?

Love,
Miles, London

Dear Miles,

> ☛ **Just before departure and during the flight, it is very good to recite the names of the *buddhas of the ten directions*.**

In whichever direction you are flying, if you recite the name of the buddha of that direction, and pay one-pointed attention to this, not only will you be free from danger, but also your wishes will be fulfilled. This is not only for safe travel, but also for the successful fulfillment of whatever goals you have for making your trip.

It is very good to pray not just for your own safety but for all the people in the airplane—all the passengers and crew—to have a safe journey. You can pray further that whoever this airplane carries may always be safe. It is very good to pray like that.

With much love and prayers,

Anyone who goes under this mantra gets one thousand eons of negative karma purified
May the whole family have long life, health and prosperity
May all wishes be fulfilled according to the Holy Dharma. with Love + prayers

Zopa
28/10/2005

The mantra Om padmo ushnisha vimale hum phet

It is very good to pray not just for your own safety but for all the people in the airplane—all passengers and crew—to have a safe journey.

Fear of Snakes

Dear Lama Zopa,
I have had a terrible fear of snakes since I was a child. When I was nine, I saw a smashed snake in my parents' garden, and a woman who claimed to be clairvoyant said that in a former life I had destroyed peoples' lives. If this is true, how can I get over my fear? How can I think about snakes if I really do have a good reason to fear them? How should I confront this dark fear?
Love,
Helga, Berlin

Dear Helga,
You do not need clairvoyance; this fear is explained by karma. In a past life, you died because a snake bit you or you died out of fear of snakes, and this has passed into your next life.

Some beings are born in a form that makes others afraid. It is just like that. Often, the fear is a result of anger. One did some unpleasant things to others, and now one fears the result.

I would run away when I see a snake, too! That is normal.

➤ **Think of the suffering of the snake: It has no choice.**

If it had a choice, it would take another form. If you were in that situation, you too would also choose another body, not a body that nobody likes. The snake itself has a fear of eagles. Use the snake to generate compassion and to develop bodhichitta. Snakes are very afraid, they hide themselves and disappear as soon as someone comes close.

➤ **Meditate on compassion, and you will reach enlightenment, by understanding the suffering of the snake.**

Now the snake is actually bringing you enlightenment, and you are able to liberate all sentient beings. When you have compassion and bodhichitta, no snake can harm you.

With much love and prayers,

This fear is explained by karma. In a past life, after dying because a snake bit you or dying out of fear of snakes, this has passed into your next life.

REMEMBER

- **Some beings are born in a form that makes others afraid.**
- **When I have compassion, no snake can harm me.**

Fighting Between Parents and Children

Dear Lama Zopa,
My parents and brothers and sisters are fighting terribly these days. I don't know how to help them get along better. My siblings, especially, are very angry with my parents, and I am worried about the heavy karma they are creating as a result. What can I do to help my family?

Love and thanks,
Jonathan, Hong Kong

My dear Jonathan,

• **Tell them that the happiness that we think comes from outside actually comes from within us, from within our own mind. It is the same with our problems.**

Actually, nothing comes from just outside; everything depends on how we think. Although things may seem to come from outside our mind, those are only conditions for problems to arise.

• **You can mention to your brothers and sisters that whatever harm they think their parents are doing to them, if they had not performed negative actions toward their parents in the past, there would be no reason for them to receive harm or any unpleasant experiences from their parents now.**

Remembering karma helps us to practice patience and to not get angry and create harm.

Our parents in this life are very powerful objects. They gave birth to our body, and even a little disrespect for them generates negative karma so heavy that the results are experienced in this life and continue into the next life.

Even performing some small service or showing some respect to your parents brings results so powerful that the experience of the results begins in this life and carries on into future lives. This comes from karma created with powerful objects, starting with your parents. This is one of the three types of karma.

With the second type of karma, the results are only experienced in the next life. The results of the third type of karma are only experienced after many lifetimes. More powerful objects than our parents are ordained monks and nuns, as well as arhats, who have been liberated from and are free of the control of delusion and karma. More powerful

If you get angry, it doesn't help. It leaves an imprint in the mind, planting a seed that will cause anger to arise again continuously in the future.

than numberless arhats is one bodhisattva, because he or she has generated bodhichitta. If you look at a bodhisattva with a disrespectful mind, this creates more negative karma than taking an eye from every sentient being in the three realms. If you look at a bodhisattva with respect and devotion, this creates much more merit than offering charity to all the beings in the three realms. That is how powerful a bodhisattva is. More powerful than numberless bodhisattvas is a buddha. Still more powerful than all the buddhas is your own virtuous friend, the guru.

These are the powerful objects in your life, so showing even a small amount of disrespect to them brings heavy negative results. The more powerful the object, the more negative the results.

> ✒ **Therefore, it's very good that you want to try to help your brothers and sisters be in harmony with your parents, so that they don't create negative karma with them.**

If you get angry, it doesn't help. It leaves an imprint in the mind, planting a seed that will cause anger to arise again continuously in the future. When you think someone is bad—that is, you label them "bad"—and you retaliate, instead of making others harm you less, you create the cause to receive more harm from others in the future.

> ✒ **In order to help yourself and to protect and give peace and happiness to yourself and others, the wisest thing, now and in the future, is not to get angry or harm beings back. The best thing is to practice compassion toward them.**

Love and prayers,

Our parents in this life are very powerful objects. They gave birth to our body, and even a little disrespect for them generates negative karma so heavy that the results are experienced in this life and continue into the next life.

REMEMBER

....

- **Even performing some small service or showing some respect to my parents brings results so powerful that the experience of the results begins in this life and carries on into future lives.**

....

Not Getting What I Want

Dear Lama Zopa,
I am very upset because my friend can't give me what I need and has really hurt my feelings. I feel so angry. What should I do?

Love,
Neela, Mumbai

Dear Neela,
You must practice forgiveness. Otherwise, you are not happy and the other person is not happy.

> ➤ **Let go and forget about it. Stop torturing yourself.**

Understand that this is the ripening of your past negative karma. Then,

> ➤ **Think about all the undesirable things other sentient beings have to experience and take them on yourself,**

so that they can experience whatever they wish, and visualize that all their wishes are fulfilled.

With much love and prayers,

REMEMBER

- **This suffering is the ripening of my past negative karma.**

You must practice forgiveness. Otherwise, you are not happy and the other person is not happy.

Letter to the President of the United States

····· *Below are edited excerpts from an open letter Rinpoche wrote to George W. Bush, President of the United States, shortly after the events of September 11th, 2001, in the U.S.A. On that occasion Rinpoche also offered the spiritual approaches to combatting terrorism that are found on pages 182–85.*

Dear Mr. President,

When the terrorists attacked the World Trade Center and the Pentagon great damage was done. Not only did they kill three thousand people, the whole world was disturbed economically, and many tens of thousands of people lost their jobs and experienced other traumatic consequences. Since war was declared some people have been protesting against it and clamoring for peace.

> ◆ **If people really want peace, then they should come up with a clear, practical idea of how to stop the terrorist attacks in the United States and other countries.**

The Problem with War

Generally, war is an ordinary method. It is what ordinary people in the world regard as the solution.

> ◆ **The problem is that war, even if it is won, is like a medicine that has side effects.**

It may temporarily help the situation, but afterward there will be continual complications. Even if you win the war, it is not really a lasting victory either for the country or for the individuals responsible. It is only a temporary victory. Why? Because the people you defeat generate hatred toward you and in future generations will harm you back. In the natural law of actions, karma in Sanskrit, the action of harming leaves an imprint on the mental continuum, which is like a seed. When it ripens later, the person experiences the result of receiving harm from others.

If at all possible, war should be avoided. Other means of solving problems, including seeking the advice of the leaders of all the spritual traditions, can be tried.

> ◆ **If all else fails, another solution would be to have a war without anger, something that appeared violent but actually stems from a positive, peaceful motivation.**

War is only a temporary victory. Why? Because the people you defeat generate hatred toward you and in future generations will harm you back.

Harming Others with Compassion

Just because something looks violent, that alone does not necessarily define it is as negative, because there are actions that outwardly appear to be violent but in reality are most positive, pure, and aimed at creating inner peace.

Buddhism is based on not harming others and on benefiting others.

> ● **But when a malicious being is harming him- or herself and greatly harming many others and the world, then in Mahayana Buddhism great saints called bodhisattvas, who have the utmost compassion, might choose to take the life of that being.**

They completely sacrifice themselves to happily experience whatever suffering consequences may come from that act of killing, such as suffering in a hell realm. They do this in order to benefit that sentient being, to stop that being from engaging in harmful actions, and also for the peace and happiness of others. Because that holy being sees there is great benefit for others in taking the life of the violent being, the action does not become dangerous for a bodhisattva. When there is greater benefit to take the life of an evil being than not to, the Buddha has permitted this for great saints who are qualified to do so.

In reality, even though an externally wrathful or violent action is used, it does not harm the evil doer; it only benefits him or her. There is no anger involved at all. The apparently wrathful aspect of mind is without any anger—the thought of harming others.

An example is when a child is very naughty and the parent has run out of peaceful means to control the child. The parent will then scold the child with a wrathful appearance because this is the only way to control the child so that he or she will have a good, successful future.

Terrible Ignorance

These terrorists' minds are so ignorant, unbelievably ignorant and hallucinatory. They are caught in the very heavy, gloomy darkness of ignorance without any light of wisdom. They are completely trapped in so many heavy iron cages of wrong views that they cannot even see that these views are wrong and that their actions are harmful. What they did, their negative thoughts and actions, caused so many thousands of people to be killed and so many firemen to sacrifice their lives to save others. Because of these very heavy actions, in the Buddhist view, they will have to suffer for thousands of eons. They will have to experience

The terrorists are completely trapped in so many heavy iron cages of wrong views that they cannot even see that these views are wrong and that their actions are harmful.

109

innumerable harms. The very heavy harmful actions they did to others and to the world are in the nature of *dependent arising,* that is, they arose from specific causes and in turn cause similar future results.

> ☙ From negative actions suffering results, from positive actions happiness arises; so it is unimaginable how much harm the terrorists did to themselves, to the U.S.A., and to the rest of the world.

Rebirth

Rebirth is not only Buddhist philosophy and experience; Christianity also talks about rebirth because it talks about a heaven and hell after this life, and about resurrection. No one has yet proved that rebirth does not exist, and countless people have realized, based on their own experience, that rebirth does exist, and that life does not end upon the death of the body.

> ☙ As the mind continues after death, negative thoughts also continue, so these terrorists will go on to harm others again and again without end, until their negative emotional thoughts are eliminated.

The Chronic Disease of the Mind

Negative thoughts, such as anger, a dissatisfied mind, and desire are the chronic disease of the mind and the main cause of suffering. If the people in this world do not put effort into making the mind better, into eliminating negative thoughts, then even when the body is destroyed and disintegrated, the mind, which does not cease, will continue along with all these thoughts.

This is the biggest problem, and eliminating the negative emotional thoughts is the ultimate solution—especially eliminating them by generating loving kindness and compassion, the ultimate good heart, cherishing others, and benefiting others. This way you do not give harm to others and you do not receive harm from others; you only benefit each other.

Religion Should Lead to Ultimate Happiness

I think religion is supposed to help in this field. I am sure that most religions have something good to offer humanity. Any religion that offers a complete method and path should bring sentient beings to ultimate happiness—the cessation of all negative thoughts, the afflicted emotional mind, including the seeds of all negativities.

Negative thoughts, such as anger, a dissatisfied mind, and desire are the chronic disease of the mind and the main cause of suffering.

- **If your religion harms others, it harms you.**

In such a case, there is no meaning to having religion. It is better to have no religion at all.

Taking Care of the Mind

I have been watching the news and heard various leaders and people talking and giving suggestions. However, I never heard any of them stress the need to take care of the mind, to guard the minds of the people living in the world. It is very clear that everything, good and bad, happiness and suffering, comes from the mind, but there was not one word about the need to develop loving kindness and compassion. Nobody emphasized the need for everyone in the whole world to practice this. I never heard anyone say this.

- **I only heard the word "compassion" twice, and both times it came from you, President Bush.**

One time you were saying that America is a compassionate country. It is extremely rare to hear the word compassion in these talks.

- **I was very happy to hear you and the British Prime Minister, Tony Blair, mention precisely that you are not attacking Muslims or Islam but the terrorists. You must keep emphasizing this.**

It would be so good if the whole world—Muslims, Christians, everyone—were to develop compassion, loving kindness, and universal responsibility. The government could put special effort into this and give special education in this in schools. This way, one child can bring so much peace and happiness into his or her own life and also to the family, country, and over time to the whole world. Then, when that child becomes a mother or father, that person can educate his or her own children to practice universal responsibility, loving kindness, and compassion so that the good heart goes from generation to generation.

Cherishing others and putting effort into developing a good heart in the office, at work, at home, everywhere—this is the ultimate method to stop terrorism worldwide. Putting special effort into this kind of education, into transforming and developing the good heart, will help reduce hatred and increase tolerance and forgiveness so that peace can be preserved. Even just one child can bring peace to millions of people.

The specific motivation for doing this and the explanations of how to do it can be taken from Christianity, Buddhism, Islam, or any other religion—anything that helps the mind to develop universal responsibility, compassion, and loving kindness toward others.

Cherishing others and putting effort into developing a good heart in the office, at work, at home, everywhere—this is the ultimate method to stop terrorism worldwide.

Interfaith Meetings

It is also important to have interfaith meetings, where all the different religious traditions led by the various religious leaders come together and pray together, each according to their own tradition. These should be made available for young people as well. If the youth of this world come together and pray together, it will contribute toward peace and harmony among the different religions of the world.

America Gives So Much Freedom

I am writing all this because I have particular concern for the American people. This country gives so much freedom for peace and happiness. There is total religious freedom and also freedom of speech. I do not know why Mainland China cannot give the same freedom to the Tibetan people and others.

Finally, I dedicate the merits and I pray every day for the peace and happiness of all living beings, that everyone may generate loving kindness, compassion, and the wish-fulfilling precious good heart. I pray that they may only benefit each other and that everyone's heart may be filled with joy and bliss. I pray that the whole world may be filled with peace and happiness.

With my prayers and good wishes,
Lama Thubten Zopa Rinpoche

If the youth of this world come together and pray together, it will contribute toward peace and harmony among the different religions of the world.

REMEMBER

- The people we defeat in war generate hatred toward us and harm us back.
- Negative actions result in suffering; positive actions result in happiness.
- The terrorists will suffer for eons for killing thousands of beings.
- Eliminating negative thoughts is the solution.
- Generate loving kindness and compassion.

Who Is God?

Dear Lama Zopa,
I am raising my young daughter, Jennifer, as a Buddhist. However, at school and among her friends she hears a lot about God, so she is feeling confused about this. She asked me to ask you about your views on God.
Thank you for your help,
Joanna, San Francisco

Dear Joanna,
If you are thinking of God as the creator of the happiness and suffering in your life, who exists separately from your mental continuum, then this kind of God doesn't exist.

➤ **But if you mean an omniscient mind that pervades all phenomena, then that does exist.**

Why is God not your creator? Because you are the creator of your own experiences—your own heaven or your own hell. Even in daily life, if you practice patience, then by not harming yourself and others, you bring peace and happiness to yourself and others. If you follow your anger, then you will harm yourself and others and create misery for yourself and others.

From this, you can see that what Buddha said in the teachings is true:

➤ **You are your own guide and also your own enemy.**

With much love and prayers,

REMEMBER

• **We are the creators of our own happiness and suffering.**

In daily life, if you practice patience, then by not harming yourself and others, you bring peace and happiness to yourself and others.

Everything Is Not Up to God

Dear Lama Zopa,
I hear all the time people saying things like, "Let go, let God." It seems like a comforting way to think, but the idea of God doesn't always make sense to me. I have been told I will go to hell if I don't believe in God. All my neighbors believe that God is our creator, and I'm starting to become afraid for my next life. Can you advise me?

Best wishes,
Gordon, Miami

Dear Gordon,

People say, "Everything is up to God." They think God is the creator and everything is up to God.

But when you look at it another way, it seems that everything is *not* up to God, because when it comes to practice, you can see that it's dependent on sentient beings themselves. People say that if you don't believe in God, you'll go to hell. By saying that, they show that in fact everything is not totally up to God—it is up to you as well!

> ❧ **Not going to hell depends on your making an effort from your own side; you have to generate faith in God. Therefore, it's not completely up to God.**

You also have to observe the Ten Commandments, for example. People say that everything is in God's hands—but you can see that God does not control everything. People themselves have to make the effort to observe the Ten Commandments; they have to practice morality.

Basically, it comes to the same point in Buddhism—from their side, sentient beings also have to make an effort.

Love and prayers,

People say that if you don't believe in God, you'll go to hell. By saying that, they show that in fact everything is not totally up to God—it is up to you as well!

REMEMBER

- **If I'm the one who has to practice, how can it all be up to God?**

Accept Death

Dear Lama Zopa,
My mother died recently, and even though she was old and it was no doubt
her time, I am overcome with grief. She was like my first self, and I feel lost
and forlorn without her. It is more than grief; I feel I have lost my purpose.
I don't know how to go on or what to do. Please advise me, Rinpoche.
Best wishes,
Gina, Montana

Dear Gina,
You have created a strong connection with your mother. Because of that,
you'll meet again.

> ⮌ **Think: "Everyone has to die."**

The whole earth has a beginning, a process of decay, and an end. It has
a certain number of years, a certain number of minutes that it will last,
and then it will end, and there will be nothing left of it. Even the Rocky
Mountains, which look so solid now, will only be space at some point.
This happens without any our having any choice in the matter, so we
must accept it.

As the great Buddhist saint Shantideva said,

> ⮌ **"If there is a remedy, then what is the use of**
> **frustration? If there is no remedy, then what is the use**
> **of frustration?"**

It's useless being upset about something that you can't have. It's like being
upset that your house is not made of diamonds, or being upset that you
are not the ruler of the world, or that you were not elected president of
the country!

Sometimes we are concerned and upset because we cherished
the comfort and pleasure of having a person with us, not because we
are concerned about the dead person and what has happened to him or
her. This is concern for our own pleasure. Our pain is due to cherishing
ourselves and losing the object of our attachment.

> ⮌ **Think: "When I stop following attachment and self-**
> **cherishing thoughts and follow wisdom, meditate on**
> **emptiness, cultivate renunciation, and think to benefit**
> **others—cultivate bodhichitta—then there's no grief and**
> **depression. There is only peace and happiness."**

It's useless being
upset about
something that you
can't have. It's like
being upset that
your house is not
made of diamonds.

Rather than feeling depressed and full of grief, which is caused by attachment and self-cherishing, let go by accepting the nature of phenomena as impermanent. Things are transitory. Everyone has to die.

Otherwise it can even make you want to commit suicide, to destroy your precious, wish-fulfilling human body, with which you can achieve all happiness up to enlightenment. Instead, do something worthwhile and beneficial for the person.

> **Be generous with those who are needy, homeless, or sick.**

Even if you have nothing to give physically, offer your service to others. Encourage others to develop their inner good heart and wisdom.

> **Dedicate all your positive actions to the person who died, for him or her not to suffer and to have ultimate happiness, to eliminate suffering and the causes of suffering completely, and to achieve the peerless happiness of enlightenment.**

There is so much you can do in the world to offer service. So much is needed. There are many spiritual projects that you can be involved with, and so many things you can do to be of benefit. This way you feel so much joy in your heart. Otherwise, you just grieve and cherish the self, which is useless.

With much love and prayers,

Rather than feeling depressed and full of grief, which is caused by attachment and self-cherishing, let go by accepting the nature of phenomena as impermanent.

REMEMBER

- It's useless being upset about something I can't have.
- I'm grieving and depressed only as long as I follow my self-cherishing.

My Husband Died

Dear Lama Zopa,

My husband died a week ago. My son and I are overcome with grief, and I do not know how to handle the huge emotions of sadness, fear, and anger that keep washing over me. I am also worried about my husband's rebirth and pray that he will be born in the upper realms. I wish there was something I could do both to counter how out of control my mind feels and to somehow send love and help to my husband.

Please advise me on how to get through this difficult time and on what to do that would be of most benefit to him.

Love,

Anne, Vermont

My dear Anne,

I am very sorry that your husband has passed away.

> **You should not worry. In my divination, some days before he passed away, it was clear that he would have a good rebirth.**

He was an easygoing person and offered service for many years to sentient beings and to the teachings of the Buddha as director of a Dharma center. He was very devoted, sincere, and kindhearted.

I wanted to let you know that I performed prayers to guide him after hearing that he had passed away. In case you are worried or missing him, you should remember that those of us who are not free from samsara all have to die. Since we are born, we have to die, because we are under the control of delusion and karma until we are free from samsara. This is the nature of life.

> **What would be of benefit is if you could perform positive actions in your daily life with a good heart, with the thought of benefiting others, with compassion and loving kindness.**

By living your life with this pure motivation and good heart, your actions become virtuous even if you don't perform any extra positive actions. You collect merit from these virtuous actions, and you can dedicate those merits for your late husband to have a good rebirth. Dedicate for him not only to achieve temporal happiness but also to be freed as quickly as possible from samsara, from the cycle of birth and death, and to achieve enlightenment in the quickest way possible.

By living your life with this pure motivation and good heart, your actions become virtuous even if you don't perform any extra positive actions.

117

G

The syllable Hri

- ● Remember him by performing more positive actions for others, such as giving generously and refraining from harming others and yourself.

- ● For his benefit, try to practice patience when somebody treats you badly, insults you, or disrespects you.

If you at least manage not to get angry, then you don't harm others. When you practice patience or try not to have the thought of harming others, also dedicate that to him.

- ● If you can, think that this is also for the happiness and benefit of all sentient beings, who, like him, also want happiness and do not want suffering.

Dedicate all the positive actions you perform each day in this way. When you start to have negative thoughts, which are harmful to others—like ill will, jealousy, and so on—stop and apply their antidotes.

Your husband's passing away is a reminder to us of how precious our human lives are and for us to practice harder and more purely.

With much love and prayers,

Try to practice patience when somebody treats you badly, insults you, or disrespects you. If you at least manage not to get angry, then you don't harm others.

REMEMBER

- • It is the nature of life that we all have to die.
- • My husband's passing away reminds me not to waste my own precious human life.

Healing Self and Others

Dear Lama Zopa,
Recently, I had a life-threatening illness, and through the help of many
doctors and alternative healthcare providers, I am almost fully recovered.
As a result, I feel called to be a healer of some sort and help others who are
now going through what I endured. Can you please give me advice about
how to prevent a recurrence of my own illness as well as to develop ways of
healing others?

With many prayers of gratitude,
Mohinda, Darjeeling

Dear Mohinda,
The most important thing is having a pure, good heart and a pure mind,
so you can understand and see where the problems are. A healthy mind
is the same as a good heart.

- **When you cherish others more than yourself, you do
  not harm others or yourself and you live longer.**

- **A good heart protects you from receiving harm from
  others, and the result of this is happiness, success,
  wealth, no fear, and no worry.**

The Buddha was like us, he also had problems, but he became
liberated forever from the causes of suffering and defilements and
achieved enlightenment because of bodhichitta. That is why buddhas are
able, in every second, to manifest numberless forms to help all beings.
Each buddha is able to liberate all sentient beings by directly touching
the causes of sickness, the imprints, and showing how to purify them.

- **Bodhichitta not only cures sickness but also enables
  you to develop all good qualities and achieve
  enlightenment.**

You become like the sun rising in the sky, which all beings can enjoy.
Bodhichitta brings happiness. By wishing to free others from suffering
and trying to do that, you experience so much peace and fulfillment, and
your life becomes worthwhile for you and for others.

Love and prayers,

*The most
important thing
is having a pure,
good heart and a
pure mind, so you
can understand
and see where the
problems are.*

REMEMBER

- **With bodhichitta, I become like the sun rising
  in the sky.**

Nothing Works

Dear Lama Zopa,
I have terrible difficulty sleeping. I have tried conventional medicine and natural healing, with no success. Please, could you send me some advice?
Love,
Camilla, Alice Springs

My very dear Camilla,
Thank you very much for your kind letter. Actually, my job is putting people to sleep; I think you know this!

If you can't fall asleep, one method is to recite prayers and read the lamrim. Often, when you perform practices, obstacles arise such as falling asleep. So maybe if you try to meditate for a long time, you will fall asleep!

People in the West think that it is a problem if you do not sleep, like there is something wrong with you; but it is only a problem if it is harming your health. Otherwise, it can be very useful.

  ➤ **Anyway, according to my divinations it seems that eating meat comes out very beneficial for you, as well as eating garlic and onions. Also, you can drink the broth from bones, boiling the bones in hot water.**

These things can help with *wind imbalance*.

  ➤ **The best thing to do is the practice of the Thirty-five Buddhas: prostrations and recitation.**

If you do this as much as possible, it may help, because it purifies your negative karma and creates the cause for you to achieve enlightenment. You can do it in the morning or evening, whichever is best.

I will also make prayers for you.

With much love and prayers,

People in the West think that it is a problem if you do not sleep, like there is something wrong with you; but it is only a problem if it is harming your health.

REMEMBER

• **Practicing the Thirty-five Buddhas will help.**

Practice Rejoicing

Dear Lama Zopa,
I am trying to decide whether to go to Australia to visit my ex-husband and
his new wife. I am worried I may feel jealous, and I am afraid of how he
might treat me. You may remember that we had some rough times together.
He lives a long way away from me now, and I don't feel confident I will be
able to handle the situation wisely when I am not on my own ground. They
have invited me, but I don't know if it's a good idea to go.

Love,
Jackie, Munich

Dear Jackie,
I suggest you go to Australia and see how things are. While you are there,

- Practice patience,

- Practice rejoicing, and

- Practice giving.

- **Especially rejoice that your ex-husband has found a new wife, someone who makes him happy.**

In your heart, you should feel not your own happiness, but
his happiness, as much as possible. Rejoice. Remember that your ex-
husband was with you for many years, dedicating his life to taking care
of you, while you were going through difficulties. He took care of you
with all his heart, giving you the opportunity to practice Dharma.

- **This is the greatest opportunity for you to practice. It is the greatest challenge.**

So, always practice rejoicing and feeling happiness for sentient
beings if they have found Dharma, freedom, wealth, education, or other
good things. This keeps your mind satisfied and helps your body, too,
such as your blood pressure.

We always need to practice rejoicing.

With much love and prayers,

Always practice
rejoicing and
feeling happiness
for sentient beings
if they have
found Dharma,
freedom, wealth,
education, or other
good things. This
keeps your mind
satisfied.

REMEMBER

- **Rejoicing in the happiness of others helps my mind and also helps my body, such as my blood pressure.**

Avoid Killing Animals

Dear Lama Zopa,

In my family, it is a tradition to go hunting for sport. Since I've started studying Buddhist teachings, I've decided not to participate in my family's hunting trips. But they argue that animals don't have feelings. I have tried to explain why we should have compassion for their suffering, but I haven't been very convincing.

Best wishes,
Colin, Auckland

Dear Colin,

➤ **Animals have feelings. They have the same type of minds as we do and also want to be happy, like we do.**

For example, if you suddenly touch an animal, it is immediately frightened. We get frightened if somebody beats or hits us with a stick. If somebody throws cold water on us, we feel shocked. Can you bear to put your finger in boiling hot water? You can't. It is the same for animals.

Even though they can't speak, animals show their fear through their bodies. Human beings can talk, complain, bring court cases, go to the police. Human beings can do so much; they can talk and express their fears. But animals can't. They can do nothing.

Whether other people accept your suffering or not, at least you can explain it and people can listen. Animals can't do this, but you can see how they feel from their movements. When someone tries to attack them, they run away. They are afraid, which means they want to be happy and not suffer. This is a very important point—that they have the same mind as us.

➤ **If you kill them, then you create the negative karma to be like them.**

For one hundred thousand lifetimes, you will suffer the consequences.

With love and many prayers,

Even though they can't speak, animals show their fear through their bodies. Human beings can talk, complain, bring court cases, go to the police. But animals can do nothing.

REMEMBER

• **Just like me, animals want to be happy.**

Killing Mice to Feed My Snake

Dear Rinpoche,
Recently, I started studying Buddhism and learned more about the
suffering of animals and the karma of killing. I am now faced with a
dilemma. Several years ago, I bought a pet snake and, as you might know,
snakes usually only eat mice. On one hand, if I don't feed my snake, it will
die. On the other hand, if I feed my snake, the mice die. I don't know what
to do because either way, a sentient being is killed.

> *Please give me some advice about how to handle this situation from*
a Buddhist perspective.

Best wishes,
Mike, Boston

My very dear Mike,
I have something to talk to you about, heart to heart, regarding the
suffering of animals.

> ↪ **As you love the snake you must also love the mice. The**
> **mice are also looking for happiness and don't want to**
> **suffer. Like the snake, the mice need love from you and**
> **want help from you.**

Also, the teachings of the Buddha talk about the karma of killing.
If you kill one sentient being, then for five hundred lifetimes you will be
killed by others. This is the result of one negative karma of killing. This
is explained by the fact that karma is expandable. If you plant one Bodhi
tree seed the size of the tip of your finger, then from that comes many
thousands of branches. All of that comes from one seed. Huge trees all
grow from small seeds. So, you can get extremely large results from one
small cause.

In terms of our inner evolution, the effect is much greater. Not
only does one suffer for many lifetimes, but the negative karma of
killing obscures the mind. It becomes an obstacle to developing loving
kindness and compassion for living beings, to developing the altruistic
mind to attain enlightenment in order to liberate sentient beings, and
to achieving liberation by removing the gross and subtle obscurations
and therefore to achieving enlightenment. Therefore, we can't do perfect
work for sentient beings by freeing them from suffering and bringing
them to enlightenment.

All of this comes from negativity such as killing. Because the

If you plant one
Bodhi tree seed the
size of the tip of
your finger, then
from that comes
many thousands of
branches. So, you
can get extremely
large results from
one small cause.

motivation is nonvirtuous, then the action becomes nonvirtuous, negative karma. This obscures the mind, and then it is difficult to see the reality, the ultimate nature of the "I," and the nature of one's own mind. One is unable to realize this.

So, if you have to take care of the snake, and the snake doesn't eat vegetarian food, you have to engage in killing. That is discriminating. If you let the snake go, it will kill other animals. The solution, either way, is problematic. Nevertheless,

1. Probably the best thing is for you to let the snake go and to pray for its higher rebirth.

2. You can recite prayers and mantras so the snake can hear them. It would be good, according to my divinations, to recite the mantra of Maitreya Buddha. Reciting this mantra would be most beneficial for all beings, not just your snake.

3. Reciting the Medicine Buddha mantra every day frees you from all suffering and brings every benefit, including success in this life, up to enlightenment.

4. Another mantra to recite is the *Stainless Pinnacle* mantra, one of the Five Powerful Mantras for Liberating Sentient Beings from the Lower Realms.

If you have to take care of the snake, and the snake doesn't eat vegetarian food, you have to engage in killing. That is discriminating. If you let the snake go, it will kill other animals. The solution, either way, is problematic.

5. When you have time it is good to recite *The Heart Sutra*, the whole text. If not, then just recite the mantra.

6. Also, to help guide you on the foundation of the path to liberation and enlightenment, it is good to read any of the short lamrim prayers to plant the seed of the whole path.

7. Another way to benefit animals is to take them around holy objects, such as statues, stupas, and scriptures, especially those containing relics and mantras. Take your snake around these holy objects as much as you can.

   Make prayers to achieve bodhichitta for the snake and all sentient beings.

   Make a prayer to realize emptiness.

   Recite: "In all my lives, may I never be separated from the victorious one, Lama Tsongkhapa, acting in person as the Mahayana guru. May I, my family, friends, and all other sentient beings never turn aside, even for an instant, from the excellent path praised by the victorious ones."

   Pray that the snakes and all beings, when they die, are immediately born in a pure land or obtain a precious human rebirth, meet a perfectly qualified Mahayana guru, practice the path, and obtain all realizations. It is good to do this for anyone for whom you want to pray.

   Then it is excellent to dedicate the merits to the animals.

8. Practice not harming others and benefiting them as much as you can.

9. You can do meditation practice to purify negative karma and pray for higher rebirths.

10. You can chant the other four of the Five Powerful Mantras and dedicate them to the higher rebirth of your snake and all animals and to their meeting the Dharma.

The best solution is to develop your mind on the path as quickly as possible, to liberate yourself from karma and delusion, enter the Mahayana path, and eliminate the subtle defilements so you have

The best solution is to develop your mind on the path as quickly as possible, to liberate yourself from karma and delusion, enter the Mahayana path, and eliminate the subtle defilements so you have omniscient mind and are able to read all sentient beings' minds.

omniscient mind and are able to read all sentient beings' minds. You are able to see their karma, wishes, characteristics, level of intelligence, and are able to see directly all the methods to help them.

If you liberate yourself and don't have to reincarnate, then there is so much relief for sentient beings, so many sentient beings don't have to suffer. You are liberated from samsara, and you are freeing other beings from having to suffer. By revealing methods, especially by revealing Dharma, you can liberate many beings and bring them to enlightenment.

> ◆ Meditate on the fact that all happiness depends on so many sentient beings.

For example, when a house is built, many worms and ants have to be killed. Many hardships are experienced by those beings. Again, for food and clothing, many beings have to be killed. For one plate of rice, so many beings have to be killed. It is the same with our clothes made of silk or animal skins. Many beings have to suffer for our comfort and survival.

The conclusion is that we can do practices now to liberate these animals from the realms of suffering. This is the solution, so that they don't have to suffer for a long time through killing each other. We should focus on this method to liberate these beings as much as possible so they don't have to suffer. This is only possible through practicing Dharma.

You can reveal the wisdom of Dharma and educate other people in this way. This brings peace and happiness to oneself and others. It is good to know more how to benefit others, how to fully liberate them, how to achieve a good rebirth in your next life, liberation from samsara, and also full enlightenment. You and others don't have to be born in the lower realms. Even if they aren't liberated from suffering and its causes and don't get enlightened in this lifetime, they can still achieve all the causes for enlightenment in the future.

So please practice compassion for others. From that comes not harming others and the thought to benefit others. Since you are a good-hearted, good-natured person, this is my humble advice to you.

Finally:

11. It would be much better to buy meat from a shop for your snake. You could try to disguise it as a mouse. Although the snake would still get some karma of killing, it would not be complete.

12. Also, if you give a toy mouse to your snake, he might learn that mice are no longer edible, and maybe he will not want to eat them any more.

So, please practice compassion for others. From that comes not harming others and the thought to benefit others. Since you are a good-hearted, good-natured person, this is my humble advice to you.

This is one small example of how you can benefit them. I hope you don't collapse or faint, overwhelmed by all this advice!

With much love and prayer,

REMEMBER

- Negative actions bring suffering and positive actions bring happiness.
- Karma multiplies: small seeds bring big fruits.
- My snake and the mice all want to be happy and not suffer.

I hope you don't collapse or faint, overwhelmed by all this advice!

Purifying Killing the Ants

Dear Lama Zopa,
I killed fifty small ants on my balcony and regretted the act immediately afterward. I am writing to confess what I have done and to say I plan to take the eight Mahayana precepts, one day for each ant I have killed.

Love,
Jeanie, Hong Kong

My very dear Jeanie,
Thank you very much for your kind letter. It is amazing what you want to offer back to those ants. It is incredible! The thought to take precepts for each ant would not have come into my head.

I am sure all the ants will jump up and down and clap their hands and have a party for you when you finish, wishing for you to receive all happiness.

I put my hands together at my heart thanking you very, very much on behalf of all the ants.

Big love and prayers,

Be Kind to Mosquitoes

I am sure all the ants will jump up and down and clap their hands and have a party for you when you finish, wishing for you to receive all happiness.

Dear Lama Zopa,
Where I live—on the border between Singapore and Malaysia—there are so many mosquitoes, and it's almost impossible to avoid killing them. I feel very guilty about it, as I have taken Buddhist vows and know that it is not good to kill. Still, I don't know what else to do.

Love and many thanks,
Ming-Na, Malaysia

My dear Ming-Na,

> 🔹 **You should not kill mosquitoes at all. Your body is so big, and they are so tiny.**

What if their bodies were big and yours were tiny, and you came to bite them and drink a little of their blood, because you were so hungry, but then they killed you? How does this look to you? This is exactly the same situation.

If you don't purify yourself of these acts, you will have to suffer the result in future lives, and also in this life, especially as you have taken vows to live in pure ethics and one of your vows is to abstain from killing. This is a very basic practice. You need to perform the various practices I am recommending for you gradually and consistently, to purify and to collect merit.

> 🔹 **You should also read the lamrim, the gradual path to enlightenment, not only for your own happiness, but also for the peace and happiness of all sentient beings, especially the mosquitoes.**

I am requesting of you, on behalf of all mosquitoes, please don't kill. I will be the voice for all the mosquitoes.

With much love and prayer,

REMEMBER

- **I must not kill!**

No Hunting, Please

⋯⋯ *Rinpoche suggested the following sign be used, along with "No Hunting" notices, at the more remote Buddhist centers.*

> 🔹 **Please don't hunt the animals. They also want happiness and do not want suffering. Just like you, they do not want to be hunted.**

If you don't purify yourself of these acts, you will have to suffer the result in future lives, and also in this life, especially as you have taken vows to live in pure ethics.

129

Cream on the Cake

Dear Lama Zopa,
I have recently started studying Buddhism, and so there are many things
I still don't know, and I have many questions. I have been reading on how
the lamrim takes one gradually along the path to enlightenment, while
with tantra one can achieve enlightenment in one life. So, my question is:
Which is more important to practice, lamrim or tantra? Shouldn't we try to
become enlightened as quickly as possible?

Best wishes,
Olga, San Francisco

Dear Olga,

HA HA

There is nothing, best life most meaningful life in the world, than actualizing Lamrim including Tantra, but Lamrim that makes Nyum Nyum cream on cake, actually Lamrim should be cream.

There is nothing better than actualizing the lamrim.

130

Should I Have an Abortion?

Dear Lama Zopa,

I am expecting a baby, but I have very little money and my boyfriend has disappeared. I'm not sure I am ready to have a child or that I can even look after it. I'm only twenty. Things are very difficult and very crazy for me right now, and I don't know what to do.

I am considering having an abortion; I don't think I can offer a child the kind of life it deserves. I know this is not a good thing to do, but I'm not sure what else to do at this point. Please let me know what is best to do.

Love,
Melissa, Virginia

Dear Melissa,
It is better to choose adoption than abortion, unless the baby has a serious illness or will experience terrible suffering. Even so, there is no comparison between that kind of suffering and the suffering of a hell realm. It is better to be born in the human realm, even for one day.

Having an abortion could shorten your life, too, as that is one of the results of killing.

- **The negative karmic effects of killing also include contracting many diseases; even food could cause you harm.**

- **Also, abortion is very unpleasant for the child.**

If the child is going to a better rebirth or to a pure land, that would be better than this life. But we don't know what is going to happen. It is much better here in the human realm than in other, worse realms.

With much love and prayers,

REMEMBER

- **It is better to choose adoption than abortion.**
- **It is better to be born in the human realm, even for one day.**

We don't know what an aborted being's next life is going to be.

Severe Physical Problems

Dear Lama Zopa,
I have become pregnant, but now I'm shocked to learn that the baby seems to have severe physical problems. I just don't know what to do. Is it okay to have an abortion? Wouldn't it be cruel to allow it be born and then to have to suffer?

Love and thanks,
Marie, Paris

Dear Marie,
All sentient beings want happiness and do not want suffering; this is what they want, even in the womb. Before deciding what to do,

- **It is important to know whether the child's next life will be better than if it were born with disabilities.**

- **If you know *definitely* that the child's next life would be better then you can choose.**

- **But it may be that the child would be reborn in the hell realms, where the suffering is a thousand times worse than any suffering imaginable in the human realm.**

If we don't know where the child will be reborn, then it is much better for the child to live and for the parent not to have an abortion.

- **Think: "This is my karma; I have a karmic debt from the past. In the past, this child took care of me, was my mother, father, and friend many times. This is why the child has been born to me."**

Do not think that this is "my child" but think of the child as a sentient being who wants happiness and does not want suffering.

You have a karmic relationship, and now it is your turn to take care of the child, repay the child's kindness, and offer service. When you offer service it is important not to think that this is "my child" but think of the child as a sentient being who wants happiness and does not want suffering. Thinking like this you receive all past, present, and future happiness. This child becomes so precious for you, like a wish-fulfilling jewel. So,

- **With this attitude, take care of the child as long as it lives.**

Even if the child is unable to function and nothing can be done, this is its karma. However, you can benefit the child a lot.

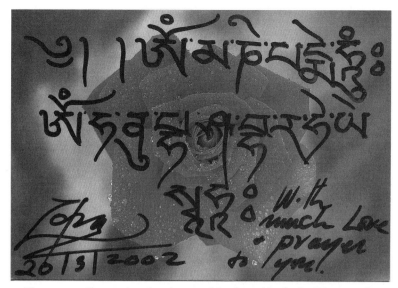

The mantras Om mani padme hum *and* Om hanu bhasha bara heye svaha

1. **You can circumambulate stupas, statues of the Buddha, or scriptures while holding your child.**

This purifies and benefits the child so much; so much negative karma is purified and so much merit is collected. You can set up a table in your house full of holy objects, such as statues, stupas, and scriptures and walk around the table.

2. **You can also chant mantras to purify negative karma and plant positive imprints, cause liberation and enlightenment, and cause all the realizations of the path up to enlightenment.**

In this way, you benefit the child so it can create merit, actualize a higher rebirth, meet the Dharma, meet a perfectly qualified Mahayana guru so as to be able to understand the Mahayana teachings and achieve the path, end samsara, and reach enlightenment. So, you see how much you can benefit the child every day.

Even if there is not much hope for the child's life, you can pray and prepare for its better future lives.

3. **You can recite *The Heart Sutra*, lamrim prayers, and mantras every day so that your child can hear them. In this way, the child hears the teachings, and thus every day you plant the seed for its enlightenment.**

Think in this way of the long-term benefits, the happiness of future lives, and especially the ultimate benefit—enlightenment.

You have a karmic relationship with this child, and now it is your turn to take care of it, repay the child's kindness, and offer service.

Of course, you can try whatever other methods are possible to help the child, but if nothing works, then these practices will free the child from samsara, from any worse suffering, from suffering karma, and they will benefit the child.

If you think that the child is not "your" child, but is a sentient being, this will make you very happy. You know that this sentient being looked after you numberless times in the past, has been your parent, and now is helping you to achieve all past, present, and future happiness, including enlightenment. This child is inspiring you to offer service and create merit for it. In this way, it is actually the best thing, no hardship at all, but such an incredible joy to offer service to and benefit this child. It gives you the opportunity to free this sentient being from samsara and bring it to enlightenment.

With much love and prayers,

REMEMBER

- The baby might be reborn in the hell realms, where the suffering is much worse than any suffering in the human realm.
- There are ways to help the child even in the womb.
- I must think of the long-term benefits, the happiness of future lives, and especially the ultimate benefit—enlightenment.

Of course, you can try whatever other methods are possible to help the child, but if nothing works, then these practices will benefit the child.

What to Do?

Dear Lama Zopa,
I have been practicing Buddhist meditation for about five years now.
For the first couple of years, I definitely felt my mind getting calmer and generally saw things in my life going more smoothly. However, over the last two years, I lost my job and am experiencing a severe illness. I sometimes think that maybe I am not practicing correctly, because all of these difficulties are coming up, unlike during the first few years when things seemed to go so well. Am I doing something wrong?

Love,
MariaElena, Bilbao

My very dear MariaElena,
I am so sorry to hear that you lost your job and are sick. As you know well, it is the nature of the world—of samsara—for things like this to happen, because of our different past karmas.

When you practice Dharma, serving others from the heart, then very heavy past negative karmas are purified in this life. The karma to be in hell for many eons manifests as an undesirable thing, such as sickness or difficulties in this life.

Also,

- ➤ Think: "I have been successful, in that all my past prayers to receive the suffering of others are having their result now. I am an extremely fortunate person, the most fortunate person."

With big love and prayer,

When you practice Dharma, serving others from the heart, then very heavy past negative karmas are purified in this life.

REMEMBER

- It's natural for bad things to happen.

Using Difficult Situations for the Best

..... Rinpoche wrote the following letter to the American businesswoman, Martha Stewart, when she was in prison.

My very dear Martha,

I hope you are doing well and that you are happy. You can learn a lot from your present situation in prison by looking at it in a positive way. Normally, you don't have the opportunity to learn this, by not being in such a situation.

> ● **Especially, you can learn to have courage and develop your full potential. In this way, you can overcome all sufferings and their causes, including the cycle of birth, death, old age, and sickness.**

You can achieve peerless happiness and full enlightenment. Not only that, you can cause so many other living beings to have perfect happiness and bring them from happiness to happiness, to the peerless happiness of full enlightenment, by liberating them from all the sufferings of cyclic existence—samsara—including the causes of negative emotional thoughts and their actions—karma.

I have seen you so many times on television and thought that I would like to send you some meditation books for you to read in prison, as you have a lot of time to analyze things, to look within yourself, to study your life, to explore change, and to achieve freedom, inner freedom, which is most important, because then you have freedom over all external things.

At other times, your life must be extremely busy, so you may not have much time to really meditate or analyze.

> ● **So this situation you are in now is like being alone in retreat, where you have space to think about your life, qualities, mistakes, and you can see deeper into your own life. Through that, you can benefit others more deeply and bring more peace and happiness to others.**

My name is *Lawudo Lama;* usually people call me Lama Zopa. I bear the name of an incarnate lama. I guess this is from some merit, positive actions, committed in past lives, and this is the result. I was born in the Himalayan Mountains, near Mount Everest. That's why I am sending you this picture of Mount Everest. Hopefully, one day you can visit there; it is a totally different world.

You can learn a lot from your present situation in prison by looking at it in a positive way.

On one side of Mount Everest is Nepal and on the other side is Tibet. In ancient times, many great yogis achieved high attainments in these places. Many holy beings meditated in the caves in these areas and were liberated there.

- **Liberation does not mean you become nothingness; it does not mean that you disappear.**

Not only does your body not disappear, but your mind also does not disappear. It does not mean that your mind becomes nonexistent; it is not like that. Liberation means you achieve total control over your body and mind, not only the *gross body and mind* but even the *extremely subtle* ones. You are free from all the gross and subtle delusions, or wrong concepts, and their actions (karma).

- **You are liberated from the sufferings of rebirth, old age, sickness, and death, as well as from the suffering of pain and the suffering of change.**

This latter refers to temporal, samsaric pleasures, which are derived from delusion and karma and which are suffering in their basic nature. If you analyze samsaric pleasures you discover that they are only suffering, just like a hallucination; they only appear as pleasure because of our ignorance.

Not only that, liberation also means you become liberated totally

If you analyze samsaric pleasures you discover that they are only suffering, just like a hallucination; they only appear as pleasure because of our ignorance.

137

from the aggregates (the body and mind), whose nature is suffering, because they are contaminated by the seed of delusion. This seed is the foundation for the sufferings of change and pain.

I try to help a little bit in the world, teaching meditations on the nature of phenomena and cause and effect, showing which effects come from which causes.

From positive causes comes happiness and from negative causes comes suffering.

I try to emphasize ethics and also teach compassion in order to alleviate the suffering of living beings, and to bring them ultimate, everlasting, peerless full enlightenment, the completely liberated state, in which we have eliminated all the mistakes of mind, gross and subtle, and have a complete, full understanding, and all realizations. With this one is able to do perfect work for so many living beings and bring them perfect, peerless bliss and full enlightenment.

Please enjoy life with a good heart and have a liberating and enlightening journey with these books.

With much love and prayers,

REMEMBER

- Liberation means one achieves total control over one's body and mind.
- If I analyze samsaric pleasures I discover that they are only suffering, just like a hallucination; they only appear as pleasure because of my ignorance.

I try to emphasize ethics and also teach compassion in order to alleviate the suffering of living beings.

Increasing Wealth

Dear Lama Zopa,
I have been having financial difficulties. My business is suddenly going
downhill and I don't know why. Random problems seem to be ruining
everything, even though I think that I am well situated to succeed and
that my business model is in order. I am going to perform the Jambhala
practice, which you recommended, to get past the obstructions that seem to
be blocking everything. Would you please advise me as how to best perform
this practice?

Love,
Dora, Singapore

My very dear Dora,
Here is how to do the practice of Jambhala, the wealth-giving buddha, so
that it will be most profitable, bringing you success and wealth.

**1. First, with the motivation of bodhichitta, generate the
wish to obtain wealth to fulfill the material needs of
your teachers, of the sangha, who preserve and spread
the Dharma, and of beings who lack the Dharma and
material things.**

Perform Jambhala practice to obtain all of those things immediately. The
main thing is to meditate on this.

**2. When you are pouring water on the head of the
Jambhala figure and reciting the mantra, visualize that
the essence of Jambhala is that of your teacher. Offer
the water and think that you have generated vast skies
of bliss and that Jambhala is inspired to grant you all
success, wealth, or whatever you wish, without delaying
for even a second.**

It is very important not just to perform Jambhala practice; you
must also

**3. Practice generosity and kindness toward other beings
and make offerings to the guru, Buddha, Dharma, and
Sangha.**

There are many opportunities offered to you in everyday life to
create so much merit. These are the basic causes for your success. If
someone is very mean and doesn't practice much generosity, it can take a
long time for success to come from performing Jambhala practice.

In daily life, take the opportunities you can to practice generosity,

*When you do
something for the
benefit of other
beings, each step
you take is for
all beings, so an
infinite amount
of merit is created
with each step.*

like when you meet beggars, just give whatever you can. It doesn't only have to be beggars on the street; it can be anybody. When people come to your house, offer them food and drink.

4. Use your opportunities to practice Dharma by offering charity.

Especially, make offerings to other students of your teachers, thinking they are of the same nature as your teachers. This creates so much merit—vast skies of merit—much more than making offerings to the buddhas of the three times, to the Dharma and Sangha, and to the countless holy statues, scriptures, tsatsas, and holy paintings that exist.

5. Reading *The Diamond Cutter Sutra* is also very good.

This creates an incredible amount of merit, more than making offerings to buddhas and bodhisattvas.

6. It is also very powerful to collect merit by making prostrations to the Buddha, especially if you prostrate to all the buddhas, holy statues, scriptures, and *tangkas*.

As many atoms as there are under your body as you prostrate, that much merit you create, and that many causes to achieve enlightenment.

Another way to create merit is

7. To recite the long-life mantra of Buddha *Amitayus*.

Reciting this mantra brings a long life not only to you but also to other people for whom you recite it. It also functions to purify negative karma. *Printing these texts and mantras* also collects merit: *The Heart Sutra*, *The Diamond Cutter Sutra*, or any teaching on wisdom.

8. Another way is to practice rejoicing.

Each time you rejoice in your own past, present, and future merits, they double or triple. You also collect merit by rejoicing in other beings' merit. If the level of the other beings' minds is lower than yours, you collect double their merit. If their level of mind is equal to yours, you collect the same amount of merit. If their level of mind is higher than yours, then you collect half their merit. You will want to practice rejoicing all day long, and night—just rejoicing!

You can collect merit within seconds that would take thousands of years to accumulate just by rejoicing. You don't need to prepare anything, just your thoughts. You can do this while walking, jogging, eating, lying on the beach—any time. This is a fantastic practice if you want to quickly gain success, wealth, and realizations of the path, and to benefit others, especially if you want to achieve enlightenment for all

As many atoms as there are under your body as you prostrate, that much merit you create, and that many causes to achieve enlightenment.

beings (which brings enlightenment for yourself) and liberate thousands of beings from samsaric suffering and bring them to full enlightenment.

There are also the *four powers,* mentioned in the teachings on the stages of the path to enlightenment, for collecting merit and for good luck. Among these are the power of the attitude, the bodhichitta motivation.

> ❧ **Whatever you are doing creates so much merit if you perform it with bodhichitta.**

When you do something for the benefit of other beings, each step you take is for all beings; an infinite amount of merit is created with each step. Each mantra you chant, for example, collects enormous merit.

With much love and prayers,

REMEMBER

- I must use opportunities to practice Dharma by offering charity.
- I can collect merit by rejoicing in other beings' merit while walking, jogging—any time.
- Whatever I do creates so much merit if I perform it with bodhichitta.

Why Am I Having Difficulties?

Dear Lama Zopa,
I am currently working for a charitable Buddhist organization and am experiencing business difficulties. Why is this? Is there anything I can do?
Love,
Sarah, California

My very dear Sarah,
How are you?

> ❧ **When you work for projects that have greater and deeper benefit for sentient beings, usually obstacles arise—not every time, but many times.**

You need to have a lot of merit to be able to offer that kind of service. Otherwise, sentient beings would be able to attain enlightenment easily, and there wouldn't be any beings left in samsara.

This is very important work because it makes your life meaningful. Even though you didn't make a lot of money, your efforts were not wasted. Even if you lose your whole business through serving others with a good heart, you still gain so much merit from that. If you don't earn a lot of money from your efforts now, sooner or later you will enjoy the result.

> ➤ In most people's cases, even though they may be making billions of dollars, it's all done for the self and for this life, and so everything becomes negative karma.

Their whole life becomes negative karma—a cause to reincarnate in the lower realms. This is what happens, not to mention such a life being meaningless and empty.

You can see the big differences between these two lives, one who works only for the self and one who serves sentient beings and the teachings of the Buddha.

With much prayer and love from the Lawudo Mickey Mouse,

REMEMBER
....
• **Working for others makes my life meaningful**

Your Karma for Wealth Is Finished

Dear Lama Zopa,
Through much hard work and personal effort, I became a successful businessman, owning many properties in Hong Kong and America. A few years ago, I decided to open a new business. I hired all the best people I could find and invested a great deal of money to ensure the business's success. In spite of the fact that I have done everything in my power, the business continues to lose money. In fact, I have lost many of my best properties, which I used as collateral for loans that I have been unable to repay. I am now in danger of losing everything I have worked for all these years.

Even if you lose your whole business through serving others with a good heart, you still gain so much merit from that.

I cannot sleep and am having serious health problems. I am not a bad person, and I feel like I made the best decisions I could, so I don't understand why this is happening to me. Is there anything I can do to stop losing money on this business?

> *Sincerely,*
> *Harold, Hong Kong*

Dear Harold,
It is important that you practice with strong faith.

> ☙ **Your good karma from the past to be wealthy has finished.**

When you had the opportunity, you didn't use it to create more good karma and more wealth by making offerings to the Buddha, Dharma, and Sangha, and by being charitable to sentient beings. You used your recent good karma just for yourself, with attachment, clinging to this life, so it did not become virtue, and the merit ended. This is the same as working hard, accumulating a lot of money, and then spending it, without saving or investing anything. All the money just gets used up.

> ☙ **When you are enjoying the results of good karma, you should continuously create more good karma with a sincere heart, with the thought of benefiting others.**

This way, you will continue to prosper.

> Much love and prayer,

REMEMBER

- **I must use my wealth for others.**

You used your recent good karma just for yourself, with clinging to this life, so it did not become virtue, and the merit ended.

143

Transforming Pain

Dear Lama Zopa,

I wanted to tell you about the experience of my friend, who had a routine biopsy shortly after reading your book Ultimate Healing. *The doctor put the needle in the wrong place, it hit a nerve, and she experienced agonizing pain throughout her body. She remembered your advice in the book about using your pain to take on the suffering of others, so she thought to herself very deeply that she was experiencing this pain for all other sentient beings. She said that when she did this, she was able to bear the agonizing pain. The experience deeply affected her, and she kept your book with her and cherished it.*

And Rinpoche, I have a question: Is it possible that a person whose mind is well prepared experiences so much joy at being able to take on the suffering of other beings that the pain is no longer experienced as suffering?

Love,

Keiko, Tokyo

Dear Keiko,

It's fantastic that your friend was able to do that. It is true that using your own suffering to take on the pain of others definitely helps you to bear pain and make it less.

> **The more you can think that you are experiencing suffering for others, the better and more powerful it is.**

Even before you perform the actual meditation, there is an effect just from the intention arising to use the pain to take on the suffering for others. It changes things. Sometimes when I have pain in my eyes, I try to think that I am taking on the suffering of other beings and experiencing it for them. I noticed that it helps; the pain decreases.

> **When you have a strong enough intention, it not only makes the pain decrease, it may even stop it.**

Sometimes when I have pain in my eyes, I try to think that I am taking on the suffering of other beings and experiencing it for them. I noticed that it helps; the pain decreases.

Of course, the motivation shouldn't be to stop the pain. It should be a genuine feeling that you want to experience the pain for others. I'm not sure what my motivation was, but we should try to generate a pure motivation without any thought of wanting the pain to decrease; then it becomes very useful.

> **If the pain continues, then you can use it to develop your mind through compassion and bodhichitta. You can practice thought transformation and have the chance to train your mind.**

If the pain stops then you lose that opportunity. You lose the benefit of having the pain.

As for your question: Yes, it is possible, but it depends how much compassion is in the person's mind. The more compassion there is, the more pain a person is able to bear for others. For him or her, it is great happiness and bliss to experience that for others.

> ☞ **The more compassion there is, the easier it is to bear the sufferings of others.**

It is like a mother who is happy to take on the suffering of her child. The mother sees her beloved son or daughter as the most precious thing in the world, and the child sees its mother as the kindest person. Because the mother sees the child as so precious, she is very happy to take on the child's sufferings. It is very easy for her. The more the child sees the mother as kind, the easier it is to bear suffering for her. So it depends on how much compassion we have and how much we are able to see others as precious and kind.

> ☞ **The more we can see others as precious and kind, the greater our compassion and loving kindness, and the more we can bear suffering for others.**

Please say "Thank you" to your friend. Tell her I would like to thank her for having that thought. Not only did she remember to perform the practice when she had pain, to help her to bear the pain, but even if she had died, because she had this thought in her mind of bearing pain for other sentient beings, she would have died in the best way. So please tell her I am very happy.

With much love and prayers,

REMEMBER

- **Using my own suffering to take on the pain of others will help me bear it.**

Even if she had died, because she had this thought in her mind of bearing pain for other sentient beings, she would have died in the best way.

Paralyzed after an Accident

Dear Lama Zopa,
A while ago I broke my back while flying a paraglider and am now
partially paralyzed. My condition improved after the pujas that I requested
were performed. Please give me your advice as to what I can do now.
Much love,
Maurizio, Rome

Dear Maurizio,

> **Until we achieve a high level on the path, where we have overcome suffering, death, and rebirth, we have to die and be reborn.**

If we have negative thoughts and actions, we are reborn in the lower realms. If we have virtuous thoughts and actions, we are born in the higher realms. The happiness we should search for is not just the happiness of this life. This life is very short, and death can happen any day, at any time. The appearance of being an Italian, of being in Italy, and so forth—all these appearances can stop at any time.

There are so many future lifetimes, one after another. We continue to have future lives until we overcome the cycle of death and rebirth, so it is important to achieve happiness in all those future lives. You need to prepare for that now.

> **Most important is the ultimate happiness of liberation and enlightenment, the end of all suffering and its causes, when you are free forever from samsara.**

There are thousands of other sentient beings who, like you, want happiness and don't want suffering. You want to be loved by everyone and don't want to receive harm. In exactly the same way, all other sentient beings want you to love and help them and don't want to receive harm from you. You are one; they are countless. Therefore, they are the most precious, most important ones, and you are responsible for freeing them from suffering and bringing them to enlightenment.

> **The conclusion is that you need to develop your mind on the path, free all sentient beings from suffering, and bring them to the highest happiness of enlightenment.**

Your disability is the result of heavy negative karma collected in many past lives. Those heavy negative karmas ripened in this life, so that you weren't reborn in the lower realms to suffer for many eons. Look at

If we have negative thoughts and actions, we are reborn in the lower realms. If we have virtuous thoughts and actions, we are born in the higher realms.

Green Tara

it as positive and rejoice. Since you have to suffer this, why not make it beneficial for other sentient beings? Take on the suffering of all other beings.

> ➣ Think: "I'm experiencing this suffering for others." Every time you do this, you collect so much merit, good karma, and happiness.

It becomes very powerful healing, purifying your past negative karma, so you don't experience eons of suffering in the lower realms or problems in this life. This way you are using your pain as a path to achieve enlightenment for sentient beings. It becomes a cause for all sentient beings to achieve happiness, especially ultimate happiness— enlightenment.

With much love and prayers,

Since you have to suffer this, why not make it beneficial for other sentient beings?

REMEMBER

• This life is very short, and death can happen any day, at any time.

Teach Your Children Well

Dear Lama Zopa,
I am a parent of four children, ranging in age from four to ten years old. I have recently become interested in Buddhism and would like to try going on a meditation retreat someday. But until my children, especially my youngest, is a little bit older, I feel that it is important for me to be with them as much as possible to guide them and provide a good example. From my heart, I would like to understand how to make raising my children part of Buddhist practice. What is the best thing that parents can do for their children? How can I help my children be better human beings?
Yours gratefully,
Maureen, Vermont

Dear Maureen,
Whatever Dharma you know, you can use to help educate your children. You can introduce simple practices into daily life—reciting mantras, performing prostrations, and making offerings to the Buddha.

> **Teach your child to go to school with the motivation of bodhichitta: to liberate others and bring them to enlightenment.**

Teach them to motivate themselves in that way in order to benefit others. They can do this before going to school in the morning. This makes their life meaningful now and beneficial in the future. Please make sure they do it.

> **Emphasize the importance of having a good heart and being kind to others, so that your children grow up with these qualities. Emphasize also that they are responsible for others' happiness, including insects and animals.**

If the parents practice in this way, being kind and good-hearted toward others, the children will see that and become generous and loving. They will grow up in the same way.

If the parents practice in this way, being kind and good-hearted toward others, the children will see that and become generous and loving. They will grow up in the same way.

Even though education in loving kindness and a compassionate attitude is not taught in schools, parents can teach this to their children.

> **If your children practice loving kindness and compassion, other sentient beings won't receive harm from them. They will receive peace and happiness.**

This comes from you, because you help your child develop. This is very important. Whether your child grows up rich or poor, it is this attitude, the good heart, that is most important.

If your child is good-hearted, he or she will be naturally disciplined, and you won't need to force him or her to do things. Negative activities will naturally stop, and you won't need to use much discipline. Beings who have loving kindness and bodhichitta do not harm others, steal, kill, and so forth, and there is no need for police or weapons. It is the same throughout the world: if people developed loving kindness and compassion, we wouldn't need instruments of force; there would be no harm because there would be no enemy. We wouldn't even need laws.

This way, your child becomes a good example for other children at school and at college. Many of their friends can become like your son or daughter. Instead of causing trouble for other children, other sentient beings, animals, the outside world, and his or her parents, your child can benefit many sentient beings. If you don't teach children how to have a good heart, they may cause trouble for their parents and become their enemies.

Love and prayers,

REMEMBER

- **If your children practice loving kindness and compassion, other sentient beings won't receive harm from them.**
- **Have a good heart and be kind to others.**

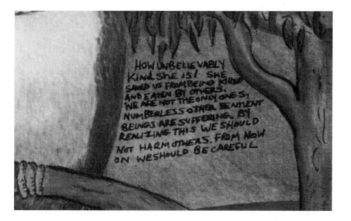

If you don't teach children how to have a good heart, they may cause trouble for their parents and become their enemies.

Pride in Good Deeds

Dear Lama Zopa,
I like to help others in many ways, but then I know I have too strong a sense of pride about my good deeds. I don't want to think that I just help people to think well of myself. Then, in a way, I would just be using people selfishly. How can I train my mind to want to help others selflessly rather than selfishly?

Love,
Rosi, Austria

Dear Rosi,
It's okay to feel happy when we help others. If pride comes, think, "I am fortunate that I'm able to help."

☙ Focus on benefiting others.

It's okay if you want them to like you so that you can bring them greater benefits, like teaching them the Dharma.

With much love and prayers,

REMEMBER

• It's okay to feel happiness when we help others.

Overwhelmed with Pride

Most Precious Teacher Lama Zopa,
I send you all my greetings and sincerest wishes for your good health. You do so much good in the world. I pray that you live long and continue to spread the teachings of the Buddha to all the corners of the world.

I would like to ask your advice about pride; it is something I struggle with daily. My mind becomes overwhelmed with pride again and again. I think that I am somehow special, superior to others. I have a hard time accepting anything other people want to give me on the grounds that I don't need anything from anybody. When someone criticizes me, my pride is easily hurt, and I react with a lot of anger. And on and on and on…I am

It's okay to feel happy when we help others.

really tired of all this inner drama and suffering. I would like to prevent it, but I don't know how. Please, can you tell me ways to handle this negative emotion?

Love,
Alejandra, Barcelona

My very dear Alejandra,
Thank you very much for your kind letter. Regarding your question on pride, this is my advice. It is important to remember that

> ◦ **Each time pride arises, it leaves negative imprints on the mind, which block the path to enlightenment.**

If you have pride in relation to lower objects—those less fortunate or with fewer spiritual realizations—it casuses strong delusion to arise and creates karma. This is very heavy and interferes with your attainment of enlightenment, which is the ultimate goal.

Pride closes your mind to realizations. Just as water cannot stay on top of an upside-down bowl, if you have pride, the water of intellectual understanding or realizations cannot get inside you.

No progress can occur in your mental continuum if you have pride. Even in worldly life, you won't get along with others. Many errors arise because of pride, including problems in future lives.

As it says in the teachings on thought transformation:

> ◦ **Think: "There is so much ignorance in my mind, and there are many subjects I know nothing about. What I know is so little, hardly anything. There is so much ignorance."**

> ◦ **Think: "My realizations are very small. I do not even have the realization of death and impermanence."**

In this way, reflect on your mistakes, including mistakes in the past. Thinking like this immediately makes you feel less proud and helps you have respect for others.

In *A Guide to the Bodhisattva's Way of Life,* it says, "I want to achieve a human body in my next life, but I create only negative karma and nonvirtue." If you examine your actions and their motivation in your daily life, you will see that your main motivation is for this life only.

Most actions are performed out of attachment seeking happiness in this life, and also attachment clinging to this life's happiness. Twenty-four hours a day our attitude is mainly attachment. This means even our

Pride prevents you from cherishing others. This becomes an obstacle to having realizations, practicing bodhichitta, and achieving enlightenment so you can benefit and liberate all other sentient beings and bring them to enlightenment.

Dharma actions are performed with this motivation, with the thought of this life's happiness. Twenty-four hours a day, your life becomes nonvirtue, and the result is to be reborn in the lower realms.

If pride arises when you see others who are ugly, have few possessions, no realizations, and so forth, the antidote is to think about the good qualities that they *do* have. That is one antidote. Then, when you see their good qualities, think "How wonderful" and rejoice. Rejoicing is also an antidote to pride.

> ➥ Think: "These beings appear to have these faults, but I never know in reality who they are, what kinds of good qualities they have, what their realizations are. I cannot see their minds, so I can't judge whether they are enlightened buddhas or bodhisattvas."

The Buddha was criticized by some non-Buddhists in India. They only saw mistakes in the Buddha. They could not see the beams of light coming from the Buddha's body. They only saw a mistaken monk. Likewise, when we think we see an inferior being, we might actually be looking at a buddha. Thinking in this way is an antidote to pride.

These are a few methods that you can use.

Pride prevents you from cherishing others. This becomes an obstacle to having realizations, practicing bodhichitta, and achieving enlightenment so you can benefit and liberate all other sentient beings and bring them to enlightenment.

I hope this is enough advice on pride. Have a good time and experience putting this advice into practice.

With much love and prayers,

If pride arises when you see others who are ugly, have few possessions, no realizations, and so forth, the antidote is to think about the good qualities that they do have.

REMEMBER

- Pride leaves negative imprints on my mind.
- With pride, I don't attain intellectual understanding or realizations.
- What I know is so little.

152

The Prison of Samsara

Dear Lama Zopa,
I have recited one million Medicine Buddha mantras and dedicated them
to your long life. I would like to request you to please be my guru.
Best wishes,
Al, San Quentin Prison,
San Francisco

My very dear Al,
Thank you very much for your kind letter.

Regarding your request for me to be your guru—I accept. You try, and I will try. You have a responsibility, and I have a responsibility. You have the responsibility to follow, and I have the responsibility to guide.

Thank you very much for reciting the Medicine Buddha mantra one million times.

> ❧ **It would also be very good if you could recite *The Heart Sutra* five thousand times so that you can quickly realize emptiness.**

Through that, you will develop wisdom. Only then can you end the most terrifying prison of karma and delusion. And only then can you be free from the prison of samsara, which is being caught in the cycle of death and rebirth and all the sufferings, and having to experience them again and again.

With much love and prayers,

REMEMBER

- **With wisdom I can get out of the prison of karma and delusion.**

You try, and I will try. You have a responsibility, and I have a responsibility.

Reincarnation

..... *Below are edited excerpts from a letter to Ted, a prisoner on death row in Texas (see page 56).*

Maybe you have heard of reincarnation. Even though this body disintegrates, it doesn't mean that the mind ceases; it continues. We have a body and mind and we relate to them as the self, the "I," which is merely imputed.

Today's mind began at dawn, but today's consciousness is the continuation of yesterday's consciousness, just before dawn. So, like that, this year's mind is the continuity of last year's mind, not a separate being. That is why we are able to remember what we did yesterday, where we went, the food that we ate, the people that we met, and so forth. The child we were and the person we are today are not separate, they are the same. You can see this by remembering what you did as a child.

> ⮑ **Even though most people don't remember, one's mind was the same continuity before one was born. Your mind did not begin only after your body came out of your mother's womb, nor when your consciousness entered the fertilized egg, and the association of body and mind started.**

Death, which means the separation of body and mind, does not end the continuity of consciousness. The mind and body are separated because they are under the control of delusion and karma, and then, again, the mind takes a body.

> ⮑ **There is always the continuity of mind. Sometimes it takes a human body, but it can also take a different type of body according to past negative or positive actions that you have committed.**

Sometimes we can be reborn in a suffering body such as that of a hell being, hungry ghost, or animal. Sometimes it can be the body of a happy transmigratory being such as a deva (worldly god), or a human body, or in a pure land, such as *Amitabha Buddha's pure land*. Or it could be a spirit body. We can also be reborn in the formless realm, where there is no physical body. Even after you are fully enlightened, still there is continuity of the enlightened mind.

In Western culture, there is not much knowledge of the mind. But knowledge of the mind in the East is very developed, profound, and vast. The omniscient one, Buddha—who is totally liberated from ignorance,

Death, which means the separation of body and mind, does not end the continuity of consciousness. The mind and body are separated because they are under the control of delusion and karma, and then, again, the mind takes a body.

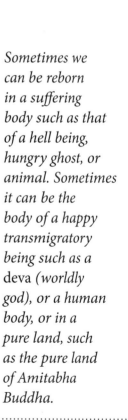

from all the errors of the mind, defilements, negative imprints, and hallucinations, who is totally free from impure views, who is beyond all this, totally liberated—explained very clearly and extensively in his teachings about the nature of the mind, the function of the mind, and all the different thoughts and mental factors.

Especially in highest yoga tantra, he explained more advanced details on the *subtle mind*. Tantra explains how all impure places, beings, animate and inanimate objects, sense enjoyments, and the impure, suffering body come from the impure wind and mind. Likewise, the enlightened deity's mandala, body, and enjoyments all come from the pure wind and mind. The Buddha has so many qualities of holy body, speech, and mind, and is able to do perfect work for all sentient beings. All of this manifests from the pure subtle wind and mind.

> ☙ Subjects such as how the world is created by the mind are not developed in Western culture. In Buddha's teachings and philosophy it is clearly explained how everything comes from karma, which is mental.

Any undesirable thing or suffering comes from negative imprints, which come from the mind, and anything that is desirable or pleasurable comes from positive virtues, which come from the mind.

The big question is: After death, which rebirth will our consciousness take? Either a miserable rebirth, such as a suffering transmigratory being, or the body of a happy transmigratory being.

> ☙ What causes one to take rebirth as a suffering transmigratory being is nonvirtuous actions committed with delusion, ignorance, anger, attachment, and a self-cherishing thought.

In this life, from the time of birth, we commit so many negative karmas. Also, from beginningless rebirths, we create so many negative karmas that we have yet to experience and have to purify. Therefore, we should prepare immediately so that we can have a good rebirth after death, to again have the opportunity to meditate, practice Dharma, develop the mind, and practice the path, not only to be liberated but enlightened, to be able to offer extensive benefit, to bring so many sentient beings to happiness, especially the ultimate happiness of enlightenment. The main objective of our life is to accomplish this; that is the purpose of living.

Sometimes we can be reborn in a suffering body such as that of a hell being, hungry ghost, or animal. Sometimes it can be the body of a happy transmigratory being such as a deva *(worldly god), or a human body, or in a pure land, such as the pure land of Amitabha Buddha.*

REMEMBER

• There is always the continuity of mind.

Of One Taste

..... *Rinpoche wrote this note on a cup for a student.*

To my very dear Georgina,
Conventionally there is me and you, samsara and enlightenment, but in emptiness there is no difference at all;

➤ **It is one taste in emptiness.**

With big love and prayers,

Bodhichitta Airways

Dear Lama Zopa,
My husband and I are always fighting these days. His business is not going well, and I have to worry about the household debts while he works all the time. He works so hard, but it is not clear that his efforts are going to help in the long run. Our personal family worries all fall on me. When he comes home, my husband does not want to hear about more problems, but I have to talk things out. His work with the business is supposed to be helping our family. He doesn't seem to even have time to think about what is needed. Every effort I make to work out problems with him just makes things harder for both of us.
> *What is your advice, Rinpoche? How can I resolve my family situation for the better?*
>
> *Love,*
> *Winnie, Hong Kong*

You can experience these problems on behalf of all sentient beings who have relationship problems, whose problems are 100,000 times worse than yours.

My very dear Winnie,
If your marriage is not working well, maybe you should marry the buddhas and the deities! What do you think about that? I guess you can still argue with the deity, but that means you have to see the deity first. The best thing is when you become the deity. That is the best marriage. Then it is goodbye to all sufferings and defilements.

In the meantime, until that happens, while you are with your husband, just change your mind when problems arise. This means accepting the experience in the opposite way.

- **Label it differently by saying, "This is fantastic, this is great."**

Why is it so fantastic? Because you can experience these problems on behalf of all sentient beings who have relationship problems, whose problems are 100,000 times worse than yours. You can experience these problems on behalf of all those who will have relationship problems in the future as well as those experiencing them now.

- **Think: "I take all their relationship problems on myself and experience them myself."**

You absorb those problems into your ego, which is what causes you all your problems. You extinguish your ego like an enemy, and it becomes nonexistent.

It is very good to think like this from time to time.

- **Perform the visualization of taking on the sufferings of others and giving your happiness and your past, present, and future merits to all the beings of the six realms and the beings in the *intermediate state*.**

- **The rest of the time, when relationship or other problems arise for you, think immediately, "I am experiencing this on behalf of all sentient beings."**

Each time you do this, you collect enormous amounts of merit and good fortune. This is the best cause for achieving enlightenment and liberating numberless sentient beings from suffering and its causes, bringing them all to enlightenment, including your husband.

- **This is the way to enjoy your life and experience its problems with happiness.**

You are achieving the best result and profiting from this experience. When you perform this practice, you will really appreciate your husband and feel his kindness in the depths of your heart. You will see that he is very precious. When you see the benefits of this practice and you come to like it, you will want to achieve this result. The reason we like money is because of what we can do with money. In the same way, you can achieve limitless benefit by experiencing these problems. Without him, this would not be possible. He is giving you this opportunity.

When you perform this practice, you will really appreciate your husband and feel his kindness in the depths of your heart. You will see that he is very precious.

➣ **Please enjoy this practice. When you perform it, you will feel like you are not of this earth. You will be flying with Bodhichitta Airways**

not with Lufthansa or British Airways. Other airlines have the potential of crashing, but there is no such possibility with Bodhichitta Airways. It is the opposite. Bodhichitta Airways is the safest airline.

Love and prayers,

REMEMBER

• **I can experience these problems on behalf of all sentient beings who have relationship problems.**

How to Make a Relationship Useful

Dear Lama Zopa,
The Buddha's teachings seem to suggest that it is impossible to be in an intimate relationship with someone, such as with a partner, without tremendous attachment. I am afraid that in my case it is proving to be true. I love my partner very much, but my attachment to him often causes me to be jealous of his friends and angry for no reason. We are both quite stubborn and don't want to give in to the other person, so we end up fighting a lot, causing each other a great deal of unhappiness. Sometimes I think I should give up and become a nun! At the same time, I think there could be a lot to learn from being with him. I would like some advice regarding how to have a good relationship and how to make the relationship most supportive for Dharma practice.

Many thanks,
Rowena, Melbourne

Other airlines have the potential of crashing, but there is no such possibility with Bodhichitta Airways. Bodhichitta Airways is the safest airline.

Dear Rowena,
Not everybody can be a monk or nun, and not everybody can live in celibacy. But,

➣ **As a couple living together, both of you can decide to use your life to benefit other sentient beings.**

I think it's very important to have that basic motivation to serve others. If you have that motivation, then you can do many, many good things together, for others. So if you are living that lifestyle, try to make your life as beneficial as you can, however much you are able.

There must be this motivation on both sides. Your own pleasure and comfort is not the first thing. The first thing is to benefit others, to act for the happiness of other sentient beings, not for your own happiness and comfort with your companion. This is the attitude you should have. Then there can be a lot of peace and happiness. You can help each other grow, and that also helps to develop your Dharma practice.

> ☙ **If the primary motivation is your own comfort and pleasure in this life, many problems can arise.**

Even though you are physically living together, there can be constant disharmony and fighting, always problems, always distrust and uncertainty. You want to be happy, but you are not, and there is no benefit to your Dharma practice.

With love and many prayers,

REMEMBER

- **The first thing is to benefit others; then I will be happy.**

There must be the motivation to make your lives as beneficial as possible for others on both sides. Your own pleasure and comfort is not the first thing.

Dangers of Religion

Dear Lama Zopa,
I have recently begun exploring different religions and spiritual movements.
I am very interested in the Buddhist path and would like your advice about
it and what you suggest I do now to progress on my own spiritual path.

Best wishes,
Sharina, Kansas

Dear Sharina,

**• Religion can be extremely dangerous. If you choose a
mistaken path, you can be cheated by it your whole life.**

Not only that, you are also cheated for many future lives, because
you will make mistakes in this life, and how your future turns out
depends on this life.

**• Whether your future lives will be good or bad depends
on how you lead this one.**

You might create an unfortunate rebirth and suffering in hell or animal
realms. If you have incorrect beliefs, believing wrong things are right,
like believing that there is no such thing as liberation from cyclic

*Religion is about
happiness, not
suffering. Real
religions bring
happiness and
peace into your life
and the lives
of others.*

This Tibetan letter AH is the Prajnaparamita,
one syllable.
This is the very heart of the Prajnaparamita
teachings, which is the heart of the entire
Buddhadharma, the 84,000 teachings of Buddha.

Zopa
24/10/2005

existence, then that affects your next life. It is very dangerous, not only for yourself, but also if you lead others according to wrong views. You can bring so many sentient beings to suffering in the lower realms, to hell, and to rebirth as hungry ghosts.

People tend to believe that their religion is best; however, it is extremely important to analyze this with wisdom. You need to develop your wisdom.

Upon analysis, we find Buddhism is extremely beneficial. It is able to discriminate between right and wrong, not only in terms of religions, but for anything in life. If parents have knowledge of Buddhism, they can judge what is right and wrong for their children. Otherwise, children can get caught up in the causes of suffering and problems in this life, and especially in future lives. So it is very helpful to understand Buddhism. Even if you don't practice it, it gives such a clear view. You can look at anything and determine what is right and what is mistaken.

> ☙ **The essence of religion should be compassion. Anything that harms others, such as sacrificing animals, is not good. Don't do things that harm others.**

If you harm others, other sentient beings will harm you. If you benefit others, you will receive benefit from other sentient beings. This is the law of nature, like when you plant a seed and it becomes a tree with branches and fruit.

You should pass on to others the wisdom you develop by studying Buddhism. Pass on whatever is correct, and educate them to have compassion and positive attitudes that enable them to help others. This way, people will experience so much happiness in this life and in their future lives as a result of their actions, which is the same as good karma.

Religion is about happiness, not suffering. Real religions bring happiness and peace into your life and the lives of others.

With love and many prayers,

REMEMBER

- **The quality of my future lives depends on how I lead this one.**
- **The essence of religion is compassion. Harming others is not good.**

People tend to believe that their religion is best; however, it is extremely important to analyze this with wisdom. You need to develop your wisdom.

It's in My Mind All the Time

Dear Lama Zopa,
Someone I know recently hurt me deeply on purpose. I feel bitter about this and I want to get back at this person. I want revenge. I know this is a bad reaction, but it's in my mind all the time—it's so hard to stop the feelings. How can I deal with these feelings?

Much love,
Laura, Madrid

Dear Laura,
It would not be a wise decision to react with revenge. Anyway, what they did will harm them. There will be definite consequences from their actions, and soon they will have to suffer and experience unfavorable conditions thousands of times more than what they have done, and for many lifetimes.

What they did is totally ignorant and stupid; there is nothing more foolish than that. They are throwing themselves into hell or on the sword.

> **If you harm them back with anger then it will be the same for you,**

and it will put you in danger for an unbelievably long time, experiencing harm for thousands of lifetimes.

> **But if you respond by using peaceful means, in order to change them, they will realize their mistake.**

By not harming them back, you don't put yourself in a worse situation than now. If you harm them, then their family and friends will become your enemy and harm you again, and there will be no end. That is the consequence of hurt and anger.

Love and prayers,

If you harm them, then their family and friends will become your enemy and harm you again, and there will be no end. That is the consequence of hurt and anger.

REMEMBER

- **There will be definite consequences from their actions, and soon they will have to suffer.**
- **If I harm them back with anger, then I will suffer too.**

It Was All about Me

Dearest Teacher and Friend, Lama Zopa Rinpoche,
I have been in the hell realms with my children for the last eighteen
months. At this point we have not spoken for many months. Over the
years they have been angry at me for a number of things. I have not seen
any of my grandchildren for over a year. It just goes on and on. I have
been alternately angry, frustrated, confused, and hurt by their behavior
toward me.

On Saturday night my husband and I had yet another conversation,
trying to figure it all out. Again, no answers. I got out of bed and went into
another room and just cried. I realized that I can get answers to these kinds
of questions from my own side. It is impossible to figure out the motivations
of others. However, I can try to understand my own motivation.

➤ **I went into a meditative state with the question, "What**
was my motivation for having each of these children?"

As my mind drifted further back in time, I remembered who I was
when they were conceived. I was a mess. I wanted my children to save me. I
wanted them to help me to have what I did not have.

➤ **I wanted someone to love me. ME ME ME. It was all**
about me and my needs, and of course when they
arrived, they were helpless and needed all those things
from me.

When I really got in touch with the feelings and thoughts in my
mind from that time, I realized why my kids have always seemed so
unhappy with me.

➤ **That important beginning was poisoned by self-**
cherishing.

At the moment that realization came, I felt a small explosion go
off in my mind. The realization of the torment in cyclic existence hit me
full on, and my heart filled with compassion for these beings. I held on to
the understanding for a while, and then I trotted off to bed. When I put
my head on the pillow, I wished that I had memorized "Calling the Lama
from Afar." I simply said three times, "Lama Zopa, help me to banish self-
cherishing from my life!" I immediately went to sleep.

➤ **In the morning when I woke up, the feeling of tightness**
in my chest, like dull teeth biting in, was gone.

I had had this feeling for eighteen months, sometimes worse than
others, but always there. And now it was gone. I felt a kind of peace that

had eluded me not just in this situation, but through many things that have happened in my life. I went to the text *The Wheel of Sharp Weapons* and found this:

"When others find fault with whatever we are doing, and people seem eager to blame only us, this is the wheel of sharp weapons returning full circle upon us from wrongs we have done. Till now we have been shameless, not caring about others. We have thought that our deeds did not matter at all. Hereafter, let's stop our offensive behavior."

It seems to me that this sums it up.

➤ **I am a cause of my own suffering, and it is up to me, and me alone, to become enlightened to stop this suffering for all beings.**

Do you think this qualifies as a meditation on the lower scope?

Biggest love and prayers to you, Dear Heart. Thank you for caring for me and never giving up on me.

Your friend in the Dharma,
Mary

"When others find fault with whatever we are doing, and people seem eager to blame only us, this is the wheel of sharp weapons returning full circle upon us from wrongs we have done."

Multiple Sclerosis

····· *Sandy, a young student in Canada, had been very sick for a number of years with multiple sclerosis. Rinpoche had given her a lot of advice. The following is a letter that she wrote to Rinpoche.*

Dear Kyabje Zopa Rinpoche,
I pray that you are well and that all of your wishes are being fulfilled. It is with great joy and admiration that I read of all your great works and projects—thank you.

> ● I am finally writing to thank you for your extremely kind advice about what practices to perform for my health and for the beautiful images of buddhas that you gave me some months ago.

The statue, tsatsa, and other images of Medicine Buddha are glorious, and I pray that I may make offerings worthy of such images.

> ● I find my words inadequate to express my feelings of gratitude to you. I feel hopeful that, because of all you and so many have done, I may be recovering from this illness to some extent.

Geshe Konchog Kyab from Florida very kindly did the puja that you recommended. He sent us pictures of the beautiful extensive offerings that he made. I continue to say the mantras of Vajra Armor *and others that you suggested. It is a great joy to make offerings from the wall beside my bed where I spend most of my time, and it is nice to imagine that a doorway to* Lapis Lazuli Land *is right here (when I remember).*

Unfortunately, my health still does not allow me to make as many offerings as I would like or to do them on my own, but I am helped, often by my mother, to make at least some. When Tom is able he helps me to make many more. Earlier in the year Tom was unemployed for about a month. This was nice as we were able to make many water-bowl offerings. I hope that my health will improve enough so that I can make a lot of offerings on my own. Until then I am grateful for the help that I am given.

I am so thankful for the practices that you advised me to perform. I find them very helpful. Although my mind is cloudy and I am ignorant, I have had the very good fortune to receive your kind advice.

> ● All the mantras you suggested are very helpful, especially the mantra of Red *Logyönma*. I find it to be very powerful.

These mantras and the Dharma I have tried to read, especially your book Ultimate Healing, *are truly like cooling waters that soothe the raging fires of my mind, despite my sorry state of being. They have saved me from hopelessness time and again.*

165

These mantras and the Dharma I have tried to read, especially your book Ultimate Healing, are truly like cooling waters that soothe the raging fires of my mind, despite my sorry state of being. They have saved me from hopelessness time and again.

I pray with all my heart to not be such a hopeless student and to be able to do as much as I can with my life for the Dharma. Please bless me to be able to do so.

The reiki healing that you recommended has also been very helpful. Having learned it, Tom has been able to save me from worsening on a number of occasions.

I will be sad to not be able to see you when you are in Vermont in August. Tom is looking forward to attending your teachings. I hope and pray to be able to see you before too long.

I pray very strongly that you are in good health and that you live a very, very long time and that all your wishes are fulfilled.

> With many thanks and love
> and prayers,
> Sandy, Ontario

P.S. I have improved quite a bit. I am able to move around more easily and am not quite as foggy minded as before. Many of the strange sensations in my body have gone, but my face can still feel quite tight. I am also not as tired most of the time.

Because of this illness I am forced to live without many of the things that I thought I couldn't live without before, such as being with people a lot, eating nice, elaborate food, going out, and so on. I only hope that I am smart enough to learn from this.

I also hope I did not write too much.

> Thank you, with love and
> respect,
> Sandy, Ontario

Because of this illness I am forced to live without many of the things that I thought I couldn't live without before, such as being with people a lot, eating nice, elaborate food, going out, and so on. I only hope that I am smart enough to learn from this.

Dear Lama Zopa,
I have had a lump in my breast for a while, and I finally had it checked.
Unfortunately, the doctors tell me that I do have a malignant tumor. I am
afraid, but I feel strong enough to face myself and do serious practice to
help with my cure. We have many faith healers here in Mexico, but I feel
I would like to follow your advice for practice. Please give me a practice
to do so that I can feel I am doing something positive to help bring myself
back to health.

Yours gratefully,
Juanita, Mexico City

My very dear Juanita,
Thank you very much for your kind note. According to my divinations,

- ➤ **It is very good for you to recite five malas of Medicine Buddha mantra every day. This will purify negative karma and help you never to be reborn in the lower realms.**

Medicine Buddha said that if even an animal hears the Medicine Buddha mantra, it will never be reborn in the lower realms. If you don't purify negative karma, you will be reborn in the lower realms as a hell being, hungry ghost, or animal, and have to suffer again and again without end. Therefore, you need to purify your negative karma now.

- ➤ **If you cannot bear cancer, how will you bear the suffering of the lower realms? Beings have to suffer in the lower realms for an incredible length of time.**

Medicine Buddha mantra prevents you from experiencing all of these things. It is much more precious than vast skies filled with gold, diamonds, and wish-fulfilling jewels. This wealth means nothing because it can't purify negative karmas.

One Medicine Buddha mantra is much more precious because it leaves the imprint of the whole path to enlightenment in your mind and helps you to have realizations of the path. It eliminates all the gross and subtle defilements and enables you to achieve enlightenment. With the Medicine Buddha mantra, you can liberate numberless sentient beings.

One student in Hong Kong performs Medicine Buddha practice daily. She had a very serious brain operation. During the operation she actually saw Medicine Buddha. She had a miraculous recovery. It was a

One student in Hong Kong performs Medicine Buddha practice daily. She had a very serious brain operation. During the operation she actually saw Medicine Buddha. She had a miraculous recovery.

very risky operation, and she surprised everyone by surviving. Medicine Buddha looked after her.

Also, a person in Taiwan, who is not Buddhist, could not move at all and didn't have anyone to help him. He needed to take his medicine very badly, but it was far away in the bathroom. Next to him was a Medicine Buddha statue. When he turned his head, he saw that the Medicine Buddha statue was holding his medicine, and he was able to take it. Later, he passed away. When he died, he made the mudra of prostration with his hands at his heart, to show that he remembered Medicine Buddha, and he passed away peacefully.

I will also make prayers for you.

With much love and prayers,

REMEMBER

- If even an animal hears the Medicine Buddha mantra, it will never be reborn in the lower realms.
- If I don't purify negative karma, I will be reborn in the lower realms. I need to purify negative karma now.
- With Medicine Buddha mantra I can liberate sentient beings from suffering and bring them to enlightenment.

One Medicine Buddha mantra is so precious because it leaves the imprint of the whole path to enlightenment in your mind and helps you to have realizations of the path.

Skin Cancer

Dear Lama Zopa,
I have just found out that I have skin cancer on my leg. I am hoping it will not spread and am being treated by the doctors for it. Meanwhile, perhaps you could suggest practices that I might do from my side in order to help cure it. I am already reciting many Medicine Buddha and Vajrasattva mantras, but perhaps there are more specific practices that would help.
Love,
Katie, Santa Fe

My very, very dear wish-fulfilling Katie,

Sorry to hear your news. I am sure it could be a manifestation of negative karma replacing many eons of being born in the hell realms. It is a great achievement that you do not have to experience so much suffering in the lower realms. Your negative karma has manifested instead as skin cancer, so this is a huge success, an achievement.

The following are my suggestions for practices for you to do:

1. *Naga incense puja and naga torma* on the particular naga days (according to *astrological dates*) for at least one month, best for two months.

2. Recite one mala of *Black Manjushri* mantras every day and then blow over the area of skin cancer.

3. When you perform your *Vajrayogini* practice, visualize yourself as Vajrayogini, and as you recite the mantra, blow over the area of skin cancer and think that it is dispelled, purified, including your delusions and karma.

4. Also, try to use this experience of having skin cancer to develop bodhichitta; experience it on behalf of all beings and let them have all your happiness, up until enlightenment. Give the skin cancer to your self-cherishing thoughts and rejoice.

5. It would be best if you could perform four *nyungné* fasting retreats. It's okay if you can't do prostrations, you can visualize them by placing your palms together.

This is how you can develop bodhichitta, using your skin cancer to benefit all beings and as a means to liberate all beings from the vast oceans of samsaric suffering and bring them to enlightenment.

I will remember you when I perform pujas and other practices.

With much love and prayers,

REMEMBER

....

- I will use this experience of having skin cancer to develop bodhichitta, experience it on behalf of all beings, and let them have all my happiness, up until enlightenment.

....

It is a great achievement that you do not have to experience so much suffering in the lower realms. Your negative karma has manifested instead as skin cancer, so this is a huge success, an achievement.

....

A Cure For Hepatitis C?

Dear Lama Zopa,
I am writing you because I have heard stories about how Tibetan lamas can cure people of chronic illnesses. I don't know if the stories are true, but I thought I would ask for your help. I am thirty-five years old and have recently been diagnosed with Hepatitis C, which is something I will have to live with for the rest of my life. This has been a real shock. Can you please help me with some sort of cure?

> *Many thanks,*
> *Keith, Brisbane*

Dear Keith,

> ☙ **It is better to ask for beneficial practices to perform than to ask for cures for sickness—unless, of course, your attitude is to serve others.**

In that case, being cured of your sickness has meaning because it is undertaken in order to help others.

If you want to get better in order to eliminate delusions and become qualified to liberate others and bring them to enlightenment, then you need to receive advice. Otherwise, the cure is just aimed at achieving happiness in this life, and with this motivation your action can be nonvirtuous. That means all the expense, effort, and years of treatment are nonvirtue, leading to suffering, not just pain and sickness, but more suffering in the future.

> ☙ **The normal practice is to purify your negative karma and delusions in order to help others, seeking this long-term benefit.**

With much love and prayers,

Without a wish to benefit others, the cure is just aimed at achieving happiness in this life, and with this motivation your action can be nonvirtuous.

REMEMBER

• I should want to get better in order to benefit others.

Dear Lama Zopa,
My father was strong and healthy up until a few weeks ago. Suddenly, he
lost all his vitality and strength. His doctor has prescribed medicine, but
nothing seems to help. We really don't know what is causing his sickness.
It seems strange that he has lost all his strength so suddenly with no clear
cause. Someone said that it could be spirits harming him and that you
would know. Is there any advice you can give us?

With heartfelt prayers,
Tsering, Kathmandu

Dear Tsering,
When a person feels very weak, often this is connected with harm from
spirits, and it is possible that the person's life could be taken away by the
spirit. The following pujas and the practices can help:

1. Lion-face Dakini,

2. *Most Secret Hayagriva*,

3. *Chetrul puja*, and

4. *Lu puja*.

I will ask a Rinpoche to perform the *chetrul* puja, and I will do the
lu puja myself.

Your father's whole family should perform the Lion-face Dakini
practice. If there is some kind of *black magic* at work here, then this
practice will be very beneficial.

I will also send the *protection cord* for him to wear that liberates
from the bondage of body, speech, and mind.

Love and prayers,

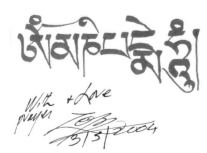

The mantra Om Mani Padme Hum

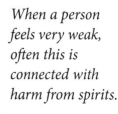

When a person
feels very weak,
often this is
connected with
harm from spirits.

Feeling Suicidal

Dear Lama Zopa,
I have been feeling very depressed and have contemplated suicide. The thought to do so arises so strongly in my mind; it really scares me. I feel like I have no choice. I don't know what to do to change my thoughts. Please give me some advice, Rinpoche.

Best wishes,
Neil, Wisconsin

Dear Neil,

When suicidal thoughts arise, there is an external spirit involved, in addition to karma.

The person starts to hallucinate, thinking suicide is the only solution for peace and happiness. But suicide is the complete opposite of that.

Therefore, you should see your mind as a baby or as a student and yourself as the teacher.

Don't listen to your baby mind. It's very dangerous.

Any time you are faced with a choice, before you follow your mind, analyze whether the shortcomings of an action are greater than the benefits, and do whatever has the greatest benefit or at least greater benefit and fewer shortcomings. If you don't analyze, it can be very dangerous.

Think: "how incredibly meaningful this perfect human body is. If I wish to achieve the ultimate happiness of the sorrowless state, I can achieve it".

Why? Because with this perfect human body, you can practice the path of the three higher trainings (morality, concentration, and wisdom) and achieve the sorrowless state in your future lives—or even in this life.

Suicide merely replaces one contaminated body with another. When a suicidal thought arises, don't follow it. Ignore it. Let it disappear, like a wind passing through.

With much love and prayers,

When a suicidal thought arises, don't follow it. Ignore it. Let it disappear, like a wind passing through.

REMEMBER

• **My human life is so precious.**

Blamed for Harming a Child

Dearest Lama Zopa Rinpoche,
I prostrate to the feet of the Spiritual Teacher Lama Zopa Rinpoche.

I am a member of a Dharma center in Spain, and I am now studying the "Discovering Buddhism" course. In this time I have had the great fortune of receiving teachings from qualified teachers and coming closer to and deepening my study of the Dharma, for which I am infinitely grateful to the teachers, the center, and all the people working for it.

I am addressing my dear teacher Lama Zopa Rinpoche because I am going through a difficult time in my life. I work as a nurse and have been doing it for twenty years with dedication, taking care of the sick.

Four years ago, the parents of a baby whom I vaccinated with an injection accused me of harming the child's leg. Even though all the specialists' reports are in my favor, and I can assure my teacher that I am not the one who caused the problem that the child is suffering from, the result is that they are taking me to court and asking for twenty-six months of prison, two years of disqualification from work and payment, and $450,000 in compensation.

I understand that the obstacles are not such obstacles if one opens to the experience without fear or resentment, not rejecting it. And I understand that this can be an opportunity to purify my mind of the delusions from past karma generated.

I know that my precious guru has more important matters to attend to and that my suffering is minimal compared to other beings'. However, I am requesting you to remember me and my family in your prayers so that these obstacles may be removed, so that I may not be condemned for an action that I have not done in this life, and so that I may never be distant from the Dharma.

Best wishes,
Fernanda, Barcelona

My very dear Fernanda,
Thank you very much for your kind letter. I am making prayers for you and your family.

> ✎ **I checked and it would be very good if you could recite *The Diamond Cutter Sutra* eight times.**

If you are able to recite it more that is even better, but please do at least eight recitations.

S

In Italy, a Dharma student who was a medical doctor explained that she had been treating a pregnant mother, but something went wrong and the baby died before birth. Then the mother sued her for negligence. The doctor told me that there was no way she was negligent; it was just something unavoidable. Anyway, the case had to go to court, and the doctor was very, very anxious. She knew that she was completely innocent but was quite sure that since it involved a medical hearing, she would be fined. She kept thinking, "You never know what karma could ripen, even though I'm innocent in this case."

It came out in my divinations for her to recite *The Diamond Cutter Sutra* eight times. She received this information the evening before her court appearance. She had a lot of faith and devotion. She immediately went on the Internet, found *The Diamond Cutter Sutra,* downloaded it, and recited it eight times throughout the night. The next morning, she went to court and won the case. They said she was innocent. So it would also be good for you to recite it eight times, but you can do more.

> ⮞ **It is extremely important that when you recite it, you don't just dedicate it to the court case, with the motivation to not be sued or to win the suit. Instead, have the motivation of liberating so many sentient beings from the ocean of samsara and its causes and bringing them to the highest enlightenment.**

For that reason, one needs to achieve enlightenment oneself, especially the wisdom realizing emptiness.

> ⮞ **It would also be good for you to recite four malas of the *Black Court Case mantra* each day until the court case finishes.**

Please make your life most meaningful with the thought of bodhichitta and meditating on the stages of the path to enlightenment.

With much love and prayers,

She had a lot of faith and devotion. She immediately went on the Internet, found The Diamond Cutter Sutra, downloaded it, and recited it eight times throughout the night. The next morning, she went to court and won the case.

REMEMBER

• **Make my life meaningful by meditating on the stages of the path to enlightenment.**

Suing Another

Dear Lama Zopa,

I am having a great deal of legal troubles at the moment. I am spending a lot of time and money on two lawsuits and am becomingly increasingly frustrated because I don't know if it's worth the energy to follow through on them.

In one case, I have invested a large amount of money with a Japanese firm. A person produced false documents indicating that the money had been invested, and then disappeared with the money. I tried to sue the company, but it denied any responsibility. A lawyer has spent several years pursuing the case, and still there is no result. If I drop the case, I will owe $180,000 in legal fees. Should I continue or drop the case?

In the second case, I lent a large sum of money to a company that has declined to repay the loan. I have taken the company to court and been awarded a judgment in my favor, but the company still has not returned the money. Should I pursue further legal action to force them to pay me back?

Love,
Glindy, Boston

Dear Glindy,
Generally, a Buddhist should not sue other people, but it depends on the circumstances. Suing has to be of benefit to others.

1. **In the first case, my divinations show that it is better for you to sue. If you have to do this, do it with compassion. Avoid unpleasantness to others.**

By having compassion, you protect yourself from the negative karma of causing unpleasantness to others. Continue trying for another seven months with this motivation:

- Think: **"I will use the money that I get from this for the benefit of sentient beings." In that way, it becomes positive, virtuous, and a cause of enlightenment.**

- Think, **"I will not act out of hatred toward others."**

2. **In the second case, my divinations show that it will be difficult to get the money back from them. It seems impossible.**

Generally, a Buddhist should not sue other people, but it depends on the circumstances. Suing has to be of benefit to others.

You can use this experience for your Dharma practice. When others can't pay you back, what you get from them through your Dharma practice is much more than if you received your money.

First, have the right motivation,

- Think: "I am going to offer charity to all sentient beings, offering them all the money that I have loaned to this company."

Even though this money doesn't actually go to all sentient beings, if you dedicate in this way from your heart, you collect the merit of offering it to them.

Remember that the Buddha sacrificed his life for sentient beings many hundreds of times for three countless eons. The reason for doing this is because other sentient beings need happiness and do not want suffering. To accomplish these aims, you need the two collections of merit: the merit of wisdom and the merit of virtue. Buddha did this, actualized the path, achieved enlightenment, and then revealed the Dharma, the whole path to enlightenment. He showed how to liberate sentient beings from suffering and its causes and how to achieve enlightenment by removing even the subtle defilements from the mind. This is an example of how you should think.

- If you can offer this money to the whole company as charity, with a good heart, it becomes Dharma, virtue, and charity, as practiced by bodhisattvas.

Since you are offering charity with the motivation of bodhichitta, you collect merit as vast as the sky. What you achieve is amazing. Each dollar you offer brings the cause of enlightenment. This means you collect as many causes of enlightenment as the number of dollars you offer.

- From this act of charity to sentient beings, you create so many causes for the happiness of future lives, the success of this life, and an uncountable amount of merit.

With much love and prayers,

Since you are offering charity with the motivation of bodhichitta, you collect merit as vast as the sky. What you achieve is amazing. Each dollar you offer brings the cause of enlightenment.

REMEMBER

- Charity creates so many causes for happiness in future lives, a successful life, and merit.

I Am Being Sued

Dear Lama Zopa,
I am a feng shui consultant. Recently I had a client to whom I gave advice about the various arrangements she could make in her house in order to increase prosperity. She followed my advice, but her business went badly a little while afterward, with the result that she lost quite a bit of money. She now claims that it was because she followed my advice that this happened, and that I am to blame for her losses. In fact, she is now suing me. What should I do?

Love,
Susie, Singapore

My dear Susie,
You can explain that while it is your definite experience that many people have received benefits from your feng shui work, including prosperity and so forth, nevertheless,

> ◦ **Feng shui alone doesn't guarantee success; the person also needs merit.**

You can explain that there are many ways that merit can be collected by people who are not Buddhist and who do not have faith in karma and reincarnation. The simple way is by practicing compassion in daily life and helping others without any expectation or thought of benefiting yourself.

> ◦ **Also, you can explain that you can collect merit by being generous, serving others, solving people's problems, and bringing them peace and happiness.**

You can also collect merit by rejoicing in positive thoughts; actions of loving kindness, cherishing others, and of charity; and feeling happy about these things.

With much love and prayers,

REMEMBER

- Feng shui alone doesn't guarantee success; the person also needs merit.
- You can collect merit by being generous, serving others, solving people's problems, and bringing them peace and happiness.

September 11th

..... *As the news of the terrorist attack of September 11th, 2001, became known, many people began calling Rinpoche to ask what could be done to help those who had died or had been hurt in the New York and Washington disasters.*

For those who want to help, my suggestion is to

- Take the eight Mahayana precepts and
- Recite as many Chenrezig mantras as you can,

with strong prayers to Chenrezig, praying for loving kindness to be generated in the minds of everyone, especially those who have caused this harm.

- You can also pray for their minds to change, to stop the thought of giving harm to others, especially those in the United States, and pray to have peace and happiness here and in the rest of the world—as much happiness as possible.

You can visualize beams of nectar being emitted from Chenrezig, entering everyone in the United States, especially those who have died or have been hurt, and also entering everyone in the world, purifying all the pain, sicknesses, and negative thoughts of harm, and all the suffering, including war. War is just one of the oceans of suffering of samsara. Perform this practice while meditating on bodhichitta. Without question, that is very important.

These practices are also good for anyone to do at any time. Without war, cancer, and so on, death will still come, and can come unexpectedly. There is a war within our own mind, a disaster with the elements in our bodies, and, of course, there is karma.

- Delusions and karma are the cause of death.

As long as delusions and karma exist, we won't be able to overcome death. We will always have to go through the cycle of death and rebirth. Nobody has ever lived without dying.

- Of course, it is impossible to overcome death and rebirth without Dharma, which means the cessation of delusion and karma.

This means correctly practicing the Dharma yourself. This way you become free of death and suffering forever, and achieve everlasting

Preventing war, so that you never experience it again, comes down to Dharma, realizing emptiness, and developing the wisdom that eradicates the root of samsara: ignorance.

happiness. Preventing war, so that you never experience it again, comes down to Dharma, realizing emptiness, and developing the wisdom that eradicates the root of samsara: ignorance. This ignorance causes all the rest of the oceans of suffering.

> ❧ Besides these practices, there are pujas that can be done for many days to protect against the dangers of earthquakes, floods, and other such obstacles, including war. These methods definitely work, but they need to be practiced for a long time, and they need to be performed by pure practitioners, who have been living a pure life and have achieved spiritual attainments.

This gives more weight to pacify such obstacles. Of course, when karma has already ripened, it is much more difficult to stop. There is more opportunity to change karma that has not yet ripened.

At this present time, it is best for us to perform strong *refuge practice* and purify the negative karma of harming others. With refuge, it is good to practice and pray for peace and recite the *Prayer for Preventing War* composed by the great yogi and *mahasiddha* Tangtong Gyelpo, which I will send to those who sincerely want to prevent war in the future.

REMEMBER

- Pray that beings stop the thought of giving harm to others, and pray that they may have as much happiness as possible.
- Delusions and karma are the cause of death.
- It is impossible to overcome death and rebirth without Dharma.

When karma has already ripened, it is much more difficult to stop. There is more opportunity to change karma that has not yet ripened.

179

How to Get Rid of Your Enemies

Dear Lama Zopa,

I found the events of September 11th deeply disturbing. It really undermined my confidence. I realize we are not as safe as we feel. There really are enemies out there. Where do they come from? Why are they there? I don't want to live in fear, but security just seems like a delusion to me now. Is there any way to be safe? How can we protect ourselves from enemies without thinking bad thoughts about everyone? I want to have loving thoughts for everyone, but I now fear people more than ever. How am I to think of potential enemies? How can we protect ourselves from others without generating hostility toward others? Please advise.

Best wishes,
George, Hong Kong

My very dear George,
How are you? What a terrible thing happened in New York! According to the news, the terrorists planned this unbelievable destruction that killed thousands of people in those buildings and also those who were in the airplanes. According to the reports, there was a passenger on one of the planes that was hijacked who got suspicious. He was able to ring his wife on his cell phone and told her he was going to try and stop the hijackers with some other people on the plane. Then suddenly the message stopped. There was no more sound on the phone, so something must have happened. He may have tried to prevent the plane from crashing into the White House or Camp David. Instead, the plane crashed to the ground in a forest.

Therefore, it becomes very important, an urgent issue, to eliminate our delusions and anger and to transform our mind into loving kindness, compassion, and a good heart that cherishes others.

1. **A solution in order not to receive harm, like this or any other kind, is to purify the past karma of having harmed others and abstain from doing it again.**

2. **The ultimate solution to prevent people harming the world is to change their minds from anger into loving kindness and compassion, and to help them cease their delusions completely, even the seed or imprint of the delusions.**

Only then can they stop harming others completely. Only the Dharma can bring a stable realization of compassion and loving kindness, and only stable compassion and loving kindness can prevent violent harm.

After killing many people in his youth, Milarepa became a great meditator and saint, which shows that the mind can change.

> ◆ **Even if the body is destroyed, completely disintegrated, it is just the house of the mind.**

The mind continues to take different forms, so it can be harmed again and again, and, in turn, can harm people back. We go on like this, and create no end for suffering.

Therefore, it becomes very important, an urgent issue, to eliminate our delusions and anger and to transform our mind into loving kindness, compassion, and a good heart that cherishes others.

This is the ultimate solution in order not to have any enemies— people don't become an enemy to you, and you don't become an enemy to them.

Love and prayers,

REMEMBER

- I will purify the karma of having harmed others and abstain from doing it again.

Transforming our minds is the ultimate solution in order not to have any enemies—people don't become an enemy to you, and you don't become an enemy to them.

Spiritual Solutions

When Rinpoche wrote to George W. Bush shortly after September 11th, 2001 (see page 108), at that time he also gave specific Buddhist practices that can counteract the danger from terrorist attacks and other large-scale catastrophes. Rinpoche addresses Americans in particular here, but these practices can be done for the safety of people and countries worldwide.

I understand that the situation is very difficult and that the American people are very angry, but there are ways to solve the problem other than by going to war. There are spiritual means. It is possible that these terrorists can be overcome by spiritual power rather than by using military power. War costs so many lives and so much money. Even one missile can be so expensive, costing millions of dollars. When spiritual power is used to solve the problem, it saves all this expense and costs hardly anything.

> **Buddhism, and especially Tibetan Buddhism, has so many methods to help bring peace and happiness to sentient beings.**

My suggestions and contribution for the present and future peace and happiness of America and the world, particularly for protection from different kinds of terrorist attacks and from being attacked by other countries, is that various practices be done.

> **1. People living in pure morality, especially the ordained ones, should read or recite the text called *The Sutra of Golden Light.***

War costs so many lives and so much money. When spiritual power is used to solve the problem, it saves all this expense and costs hardly anything.

This is one of Shakyamuni Buddha's most precious holy teachings, and reading it has benefits as vast as the infinite sky. It

> **Brings peace to the country,**

> **Prevents harm or attacks from outside,**

> **Eliminates other problems, including economic difficulties, and**

> **Prevents natural disasters such as earthquakes, storms, floods, tornadoes, hurricanes, and so forth.**

Shakyamuni Buddha

Buddhist monks and nuns in America could recite this text for two to three years. Laypeople and also non-Buddhists who have an open mind can also read it. Then there will be so much benefit for the country.

TERRORISM

The danger to America is not only from terrorists but also from natural disasters such as earthquakes, tornadoes, and so forth. These natural disasters can be controlled by removing the conditions, especially by purifying the causes within the minds of the people who experience them.

My next suggestion:

2. There is a powerful short meditation on the Medicine Buddha that came from the enlightened yogi Padmasambhava.

The practice is to prevent catching sicknesses from others or, if one has already been infected, to be healed. I thought this could be very helpful, and it was recommended also by another spiritual person who predicted that it could be very beneficial in protecting from anthrax poisoning.

3. There is also the powerful Mantra Purifying All Negative Karma and Defilements.

This not only protects from anthrax, but it also, if recited daily, is an excellent protection against danger to life caused by earthquakes, fire, tornadoes, hurricanes, floods, and so forth—the dangers of the four elements.

To prevent many billions of dollars of damage to buildings and also to save many human beings from death, one can also do the following practices.

4. There is a practice of offering tea to the beings who control the weather and create disturbances. There is a *tea offering prayer* called "Ablution to the Eight Worldly Powerful Spirits" that is very effective. The practice itself is nothing—just reciting a short prayer mentioning their names and asking them not to create these disturbances.

5. Praying very strongly to the female buddha Tara is also very effective in stopping dangers. She is the embodiment of all the buddhas' actions, and there is a mantra, a short prayer, and a long prayer with twenty-one praises.

6. Relying upon and praying to Shakyamuni Buddha with a sincere heart, reciting his name and mantra, and making strong requests for these dangers to be pacified will be very effective.

7. Recite *The Diamond Cutter Sutra*.

In situations where ordinary people cannot control disasters, they should rely upon spiritual means and try to use spiritually powerful methods to prevent or reduce them. This does not just mean Buddhist methods, but also those from Christianity, Hinduism, Islam, or any religion.

8. Recite *The Heart Sutra* while meditating on emptiness.

9. Another very powerful method that can be helpful, when these dangers are going to happen, is to pray to the *One Who Gazes with a Compassionate Eye*. Recite the mantra, have total reliance on him, and make strong prayers.

These are a few small suggestions. The techniques are very simple, but the results can be of great benefit to the area and to the country. Other things that can be done are:

10. The Buddhist tantras are full of methods for overcoming all kinds of disasters, including war, and for purifying the causes, but of course their success depends on how qualified the people performing these meditations are.

Even if there are no Tibetan Buddhist centers in the area where the disasters are going to happen, it still may be possible for people in a Tibetan Buddhist center in another state to make the prayers.

What I am trying to do here is give a few simple examples of things that can be done to prevent huge obstacles occurring. I want to emphasize that in situations where ordinary people cannot control disasters, they should rely upon spiritual means and try to use spiritually powerful methods to prevent or reduce them. This does not just mean Buddhist methods, but also those from Christianity, Hinduism, Islam, or any religion.

- The main causes of natural disaster and so forth are in the minds of those who experience them and these causes can be purified.

So, it is very important before the cause has ripened into a result and the problem is being experienced, to practice loving kindness, universal responsibility, tolerance, forgiveness, and kindness toward others—cherishing others, instead of being careless toward them and cherishing only yourself.

Even though the methods I have explained here are taken from Buddhism, this is just like taking medicine when there is danger of dying—the tradition does not really matter, it is just a question of staying alive and saving others from danger. The main thing is how important it is for people to make use of these mantras and prayers. These practices cannot harm in any way. They have no side effects and they can do no harm to the body or mind.

It is very important before the cause has ripened into a result and the problem is being experienced, to practice loving kindness, universal responsibility, tolerance, forgiveness, and kindness toward others.

Helping the People Who Died

..... *Rinpoche made the following comments on the many beings killed by the December 2004 tsunami.*

Most of the local people and international community are concerned about the dead. As many of the people who died hadn't met the Dharma, the whole of their lives were lived under the control of their delusions, creating negative karma (many were fishermen), with no opportunities to purify even one negative karma in their entire lives. This means that they'll mostly be born in the lower realms and in the heaviest samsaric situation, suffering in the hells.

As Buddhists who believe in karma, we can pray for the people who died. Most people in the world are very sad, but they don't know about reincarnation and karma, or even if they do know about it, they don't know what to do to help. So, we can offer prayers on their behalf.

Most people in the world are very sad, but they don't know about reincarnation and karma, or even if they do know about it, they don't know what to do to help.

Can't Find a Job

Dear Lama Zopa,
My whole life I have not been a materialistic person, so I haven't concerned myself very much with money but more with spiritual practice. Two years ago, I returned from an extended trip traveling to different parts of the world and decided to settle in London. Since my return, I have not been able to find a steady job and have experienced a lot of problems finding a good place to live. I feel funny asking for advice about material success, but I am coming to understand that I need to have some basic material well-being to continue with my Dharma practice.

Best wishes,
Kenny, London

Dear Kenny,

- Make *water-bowl offerings,*

- *Light offerings,* and

- Whatever other offerings you can

as many as possible, every day. When you make offerings,

- Think: "All the buddhas are the guru,"

with whichever guru you have a Dharma connection—His Holiness the Dalai Lama, for example. Actions performed in relation to the guru have the greatest karmic effect, so by making offerings to your guru, you collect the most merit, far greater than the merit of having offered to numberless Buddhas, Dharmas, Sanghas, statues, stupas, holy paintings, and so on. This brings the quickest success and happiness not only in this life but also in future lives, including the ultimate success of liberation and full enlightenment.

As usual, as His Holiness the Dalai Lama advises,

- Practice the good heart toward others in your daily life, even through helping others with small things.

- Practice generosity toward others.

As a result, eventually all your wishes will be fulfilled.

With much love and prayers,

By making offerings to your guru, you collect the most merit, far greater than the merit of having offered to numberless Buddhas, Dharmas, Sanghas, statues, stupas, holy paintings, and so on.

On Eating Meat

Dear Lama Zopa,
Should I stop eating meat?

Love,
Tenzin, Vermont

Dear Tenzin,

I've been meaning to mention to you that it's best to avoid eating meat. Of course, sometimes people have no choice and have to eat meat. But in your case in particular—out of compassion—I recommend you avoid doing so.

> **Before eating meat, think of where it came from—through cutting an animal's neck against its will—and how much suffering the animal experienced.**

After thinking about that, you *can't* eat the meat! Meat may be nice for the person eating it but not for the animal who suffered so much and didn't die naturally.

You can say prayers for the animal that was killed, but if you eat the meat, you are still playing a small part in the death of the animal.

> **If everyone stopped eating meat, then no more animals would be killed for that purpose.**

REMEMBER

- **Think of where meat comes from.**
- **Think of the suffering of the animal.**

Meat may be nice for the person eating it but not for the animal who suffered so much and didn't die naturally.

Violent Schoolchildren

Dear Lama Zopa,
I teach young school children, and many of them are shockingly violent
with each other, both verbally and physically. I never thought children were
supposed to be this way. I don't think they were in the past. Whatever the
cause, how can I teach them to be good and kind? They seem to have a
very different idea about how they should be. They come across as hard,
as determined to act in mean ways. They seem almost self-righteous about
violence. How can I get through to them? What can I say to prove to them
that violence is not the way?

Thanks,
Dani, Berne

Dear Dani,
You can teach the children the following psychology:

> ❧ **"You don't want anybody to harm you. You want**
> **people to praise you and say nice things to you.**
> **Everyone else wants exactly the same things. They**
> **want, need, have the right to, and like to receive**
> **respect, praise, and help from you."**

If your advice to the children is constant, some of them will
change. That is the benefit. Not all of them will change—that would be a
miracle—but some will.

It is important to demonstrate things to children. Pretend to be
angry and show the harmfulness of anger. Instead of talking about it, act
it out. Show how, when you get angry, you make others angry, too. You
destroy your family, relationships, and possessions.

When you get angry, and the anger is caused by something very
small, almost nothing, the consequences can become very big. This
shows why it is so important to practice patience.

Having a dissatisfied and degenerated mind is natural unless you
become enlightened. The important thing—without using the words
karma or *rebirth*—is to teach about the effects of actions in day-to-day
life.

> ❧ **Tell them: "If you start to dislike somebody, then you**
> **are sending that person bad vibrations and feelings**
> **of disrespect. This disturbs the person, makes him**
> **unhappy, and he starts to dislike you. The effect**

Pretend to be
angry and show
the harmfulness
of anger. Show
how, when you
get angry, you
make others angry,
too. You destroy
your family,
relationships, and
possessions.

comes back to you. So, what you are doing makes you unhappy. This goes on and on, with that person and with many other people. You make your own mind and life unhappy."

It is very important to try to change children's attitude toward this life.

> ◆ Establish the concept of liking others by thinking of the benefits this has.

When others disrespect you, you think this is harmful to you, but it also has another side; it isn't only harm.

> ◆ Tell them: "If you interpret others' minds and actions as harmful, then that is what you see."

> ◆ Tell them: "You can also interpret them as positive, by seeing the benefits you receive from the way the person thinks of you—with dislike, anger, undesirable actions, and so on—as helping you to develop compassion, loving kindness, a warm heart, and peace of mind."

This is the fundamental psychology. Through this, the mind becomes stable and there is always peace.

That is the best way to teach the children.

With much love and prayers,

The sylable Hum

REMEMBER

- I don't want anybody to harm me. Everyone else wants exactly the same thing.
- When I get angry, I make others angry, too. I destroy my family, relationships, and possessions.
- Liking others has many benefits.
- When somebody harms me, or is angry with me, I should look at the positive side.

I Was Shot

Dear Lama Zopa,
I was shot in the leg by thieves while I was in Bodhgaya doing my practices.
I had forty bullet holes in my leg and had operations in Bodhgaya and
Delhi to remove all the pieces of metal, although they were not able to
get all of them. I am only concerned that I might not be able to finish my
prostrations or do the rest of my practices.

I was shot on a Buddhist holy day, just after finishing my
Vajrasattva practice. I had just begun my prostrations and was preparing
to do a long retreat. Now I have pellets in my leg, which may need to be
removed at a later date.

I was wondering whether more karma like being shot is going to
ripen, and if so what is the best thing for me to do? What practice should I
do next?

Love,
Vera, Bodhgaya

Dear Vera,
I think you understand this is the result of your negative actions
committed in the past, doing something similar to this to others. That
imprint has projected this appearance. This has become your most
powerful practice for gaining enlightenment and benefiting all sentient
beings.

> **You should use the practice of tonglen, taking on the**
> **suffering of all sentient beings,**

particularly the suffering of sentient beings who are experiencing the
same kind of suffering and those who have those imprints. This is more
powerful purification than prostrations.

With everything you experience, like pain, please make it for the
benefit of sentient beings. This way you receive limitless merit. Your
preliminary practices are embodied in experiencing the problems of all
sentient beings.

> **Think: "May all their suffering ripen on me now. May I**
> **experience this suffering for the benefit of all sentient**
> **beings."**

Many prayers,

With everything
you experience,
like pain, please
make it for the
benefit of sentient
beings.

Why Did My Husband Abuse Me?

Dear Lama Zopa,
I recently separated from my husband after many years of physical, verbal, and emotional abuse. I am feeling so many emotions right now, like depression and loneliness. I am also feeling tremendous anger toward him for what he did to our family, in spite of the fact that during our whole marriage all I ever did was care for him: cook, clean, and take care of our children.

To be honest, I am having a very hard time understanding why this is all happening to me. If karma really works, why does it seem that he always gets everything he wants and nothing bad happens to him? I feel very discouraged about my life and don't feel like practicing Dharma at all. My friends and family don't understand what I am going through and I feel so alone. Rinpoche, what should I do?

Love,
Corinne, Texas

Dear Corinne,
I had heard that you have been in a difficult situation with your husband. It is good that you were able to separate from him.

It's very important always to remember the negative karma from our own past lives. In the past you treated him the same way. It's good to remember this so that you don't get angry with him. Because you treated him badly in a past life, he is treating you badly now, and that will cause him to be reborn in the lower realms. This is how you can develop compassion.

> ☙ Think: "I did similar things to him in the past."

You can also think this way about others who harm you.

> ☙ Think: "The situation is this: I must be liberated from samsara. Therefore, I must practice Dharma. There is no other way."

All the problems you experience are teaching you and persuading you to practice Dharma. They remind you to abandon negative karma and always to generate good karma.

> ☙ Think: "I must experience problems with compassion."

This means for the benefit of all sentient beings. There are numberless others whose problems are greater than yours—you are just one person.

In the past you treated him the same way. It's good to remember this so that you don't get angry with him.

- Think: "How wonderful for me to experience suffering and its cause, and let others have all happiness, up until the highest happiness of enlightenment. I am just one person. Whether I am reborn in the hell realms or whether I achieve liberation means nothing."

Perform this meditation whenever you can, morning and evening.

Everything you receive comes from the kindness of all sentient beings. They are the most precious beings to you, so

- Visualize taking on all their suffering, with compassion, in the form of pollution or smoke. Give it to your ego. Your ego then becomes totally nonexistent, and so does the emotional "I." It becomes nonexistent because it *is* nonexistent.

Perform this meditation from time to time.

Also, meditate on loving kindness.

- Think: "May all sentient beings have worldly and ultimate happiness." Imagine giving all your past, present, and future happiness to every sentient being. Visualize that it becomes whatever they want or need, causes them to actualize the path, and that that path causes them to eliminate all their defilements.

If you don't generate compassion, you don't receive any of the limitless skies of benefit. Other beings are the most kind ones in our lives. We should only cherish and work for others. They need happiness, not suffering. It is our responsibility to achieve this for all sentient beings.

Love and prayers,

REMEMBER

- In the past I treated him the same way.
- I am experiencing this problem for others.
- I will give the suffering to my ego.

Everything you receive comes from the kindness of all sentient beings. They are the most precious beings to you, so visualize taking on all their suffering, with compassion, in the form of pollution or smoke. Give it to your ego.

Negative Rejoicing

..... Rinpoche gave the following advice after the government of the United States began attacking Afghanistan in the wake of the events of September 11th, 2001.

Be sure you don't rejoice in what is happening.

This involves very heavy negative karma. If we feel dislike or hatred toward the Taliban, or whomever, and we hear that they have been killed or destroyed, then we might automatically rejoice or feel happy.

But if we rejoice, for example, when we hear that one thousand people were killed or hurt, we receive the same heavy karma as if we ourselves had killed one thousand people.

Simply by rejoicing or just feeling happy about this, it's the same heavy karma as having killed one thousand human beings yourself, even though you are not physically taking part in the war. You didn't actually bomb or shoot them, you didn't do anything, but you get the same heavy negative karma as the person who actually killed one thousand people.

If you dislike or hate these people and then you rejoice in something negative that has happened to them, it brings a very heavy outcome. If you didn't hate them, I don't think you would rejoice in this way.

The first time I heard about the destruction in Afghanistan, when a few places were destroyed, I was not careful. The news didn't say "people" or "killing," it said some "places" were destroyed. I was not careful with my mind, not watching it, so I felt something kind of good, then immediately I noticed what I felt. After that I was more aware.

Be careful not to rejoice when you hear the news. If you meditate like this, your view changes.

When you don't meditate and don't hold sentient beings as precious, with compassion, then you might see them as undesirable and rejoice in their deaths.

REMEMBER

- **Don't rejoice when people are killed.**
- **If I rejoice when I hear that people were killed or hurt, I receive the same heavy karma as if I had killed the people myself.**

When you don't meditate and hold sentient beings as precious, with compassion, then you might see them as undesirable and rejoice in their deaths.

Glossary

All terms in italic in the entries below can be found as their own entry here. Entries not found here, which are the names of practices, of Buddhas, etc., can be found in the list that starts on page 200, Mantras and Practices.

Abhidharmakosha. A book by the fourth-century Indian Buddhist master Vasubandhu, *The Treasury of Higher Knowledge.*

aggregates. One way that Buddha divides up the components of a person, into five: form, feeling, recognition, compounded aggregates, and consciousness.

Amitabha Buddha's pure land. A subtle state of existence for highly evolved minds; one of many pure lands, each associated with its own *buddha.*

arhat (Sanskrit; enemy destroyer). A person who has destroyed their *delusions* and achieved their final goal, either *liberation* or *enlightenment.*

arya (Sanskrit; superior). Anyone who is out of *samsara:* from the first moment of having directly realized *emptiness* up through to the attainment of *enlightenment.*

astrological dates. The Tibetan lunar calendar is calculated annually and includes various days for particular practices. *See also* naga incense puja and naga torma *in Mantras and Practices*

asura. One of the three *upper realms* within *samsara;* higher than a human birth but with more suffering than the *devas.*

attachment. Desire; stemming from dissatisfaction, the *delusion* that causes one to exaggerate the nice qualities of people or things and yearn to possess them.

aversion. Anger; the *delusion* that arises when *attachment* doesn't get what it wants, which causes one to exaggerate the ugly qualities of people and things and to dislike them.

black magic. Invoking negative spirits to harm others. *See* spirit harm

bodhichitta (Sanskrit; awakening mind). The heartfelt aspiration to become a *buddha* in order to alleviate the suffering of all beings, just like a mother for her child.

bodhisattva (Sanskrit; awakening person). A person who has accomplished *bodhichitta;* a saint; a person on the path to *buddhahood.*

buddha (Sanskrit; fully awake). Omniscient; a person who has attained *enlightenment,* thus possessing perfect wisdom, perfect compassion, and perfect power: the capacity to see the minds of all *sentient beings;* the heartfelt wish to benefit them; and the effortless ability to do so. When capitalized, refers specifically to *Shakyamuni Buddha.*

buddhahood. *See* buddha

buddha nature. The innate potential of every *sentient being* to become a *buddha.*

central channel. In tantra, the main channel of the subtle nervous system, which runs the length of the body, just in front of the spine, through which *winds* and the various states of mind associated with them flow. *See also* subtle mind and body

charity of fearlessness. The generosity of protecting *sentient beings* from the fear of death. One of three charities, along with giving Dharma and giving material goods.

chakras, winds, and drops. *See* subtle mind and body; wind

concentration. *See* calm abiding meditation *in Mantras and Prayers*

deity. In *tantra*, equivalent of *buddha*.

delusion. Defilement; disturbing emotional thought; mistake of mind; negative emotional thought; obscuration; wrong concept. The cause of one's own suffering and of why one creates negative *karma* by harming others. The three main delusions are *attachment, aversion,* and *ignorance.*

dependent arising. The natural law that everything happens in dependence upon various factors; suffering results from negative actions, happiness from positive. *See also* karma; emptiness

deva (Sanskrit; god). A being in the highest of the three upper realms of *samsara,* where there is much less suffering than in the human realm.

Dharma. The Buddha's teachings; spiritual practice.

dharmakaya and rupakaya (Sanskrit; truth body and form body). The *omniscient* consciousness of a *buddha* and the forms they manifest in in order to benefit *sentient beings.*

Dharma name. A name that expresses spiritual qualities.

ego. The mistaken sense of self, or "I," that *sentient beings* instinctively believe exists inherently, from its own side. This belief is the main reason for being stuck in *samsara. See also* delusion; emptiness; ignorance

eight freedoms and ten richnesses. The various circumstances that comprise a fortunate human rebirth, as described in the *lamrim.*

eight worldly concerns. A way of dividing how we experience *attachment* on a daily basis: craving (1) to receive things, (2) to be happy, (3) to hear praise, (4) to have a good reputation; and craving not to have the opposite of these four.

emptiness. Everything lacks, is empty of, self- or inherent existence: a false essence or identity that all *sentient beings* project onto self and everything else; a function of the root *delusion, ignorance. See also* dependent arising; ego

enlightenment. Buddhahood; omniscience; state of perfection. *See* buddha

extremely subtle body and mind. In *tantra,* the most subtle of the three levels of a person's physical and mental energies, *gross, subtle,* and extremely subtle; that which continues after death into the next rebirth.

feng shui. A Chinese system for arranging and orienting homes, businesses, and other areas so that the space is conducive to success and well-being.

formless realms. *See* samsara

four noble truths. The essence of all the Buddha's teachings: that (1) life is characterized by suffering, which is (2) caused by *karma* and *delusions,* and (3) can be eliminated (4) by practicing morality, *concentration,* and *wisdom.*

FPMT. Lama Zopa Rinpoche's organization, the Foundation for the Preservation of the Mahayana Tradition, founded at *Kopan Monastery* in the early 1970s by Rinpoche's guru, *Lama Yeshe.*

gross body and mind. In *tantra,* the grossest of the three levels of a person's physical and mental energies, gross, *subtle,* and *extremely subtle*: the ordinary body and conceptual thoughts, emotions, and sensory awareness.

guru (Sanskrit; heavy with qualities). Lama (Tibetan); spiritual teacher; virtuous friend.

hell. The lowest of the three lower realms of *samsara,* characterized by unimaginably intense and prolonged suffering; like all realms within samsara, it doesn't last forever.

holy beings. A term used to refer to the *buddhas* and *bodhisattvas.*

hungry ghost. A type of spirit, within one of the three lower realms of *samsara*, characterized by insatiable craving, *attachment*.

ignorance. The *delusion* that is the root of suffering, causing one to exaggerate the essential nature of one's own self and everything else and to believe instinctively that they exist inherently, thus triggering the other delusions and *karma*. *See also* ego; emptiness

inherently existent. *See* emptiness

intermediate state (Tibetan: *bardo*). A dreamlike state of existence between death and the next rebirth, lasting not more than seven weeks.

karma (Sanskrit; action). The natural law of cause and effect: positive actions produce happiness and negative actions produce suffering. Every thought, word, and physical action necessarily leaves a seed in the mind that ripens in the future as an experience.

kaya (Sanskrit; body). *See* dharmakaya and rupakaya

Kopan Monastery. The monastery established by *Lama Yeshe* and Lama Zopa Rinpoche in 1970 on a hill in the Kathmandu Valley, Nepal, where now some 350 monks study and meditate; its sister monastery of 350 nuns, Kachoe Ghakyil, is nearby. It holds courses throughout the year for visitors from other countries.

lama. *See* guru

Lama Yeshe. Born in Tibet in 1935 and educated since childhood as a monk, he escaped into exile in 1959, settled in Kathmandu, Nepal, in 1967; founded the *FPMT* in the early 1970s after he and Lama Zopa Rinpoche, his main disciple, started teaching *Dharma* to Westerners at *Kopan Monastery*. He passed away in 1984.

Lama Tsongkhapa. Fourteenth-century founder of the Gelug lineage of Tibetan Buddhism.

lamrim (Tibetan; gradual path). Stages of the path to *enlightenment*; a step-by-step presentation of Buddha's teachings, unique to Tibet that is, effectively, a course on how to become enlightened.

Lapis Lazuli Land. The pure land of Medicine Buddha. *See also* Amitabha Buddha's pure land; Medicine Buddha *in Mantras and Practices*

Lawudo Lama. Name given to Lama Zopa Rinpoche in his previous life when he, Kunsang Yeshe, meditated in a cave at Lawudo in Solu Khumbu, Nepal.

Lesser Vehicle (Sanskrit: *Hinayana*). The lower and medium levels of *lamrim* practice, the goal of which is to achieve *liberation* from one's own suffering, the end of *karma* and *delusion*.

liberation (Sanskrit: *nirvana*). Freedom; cessation. The end of one's suffering, achieved when the *delusions* have been removed from the mind; the goal of the practitioner of the *Lesser Vehicle*. *See also* enlightenment; Mahayana

lower realms. *See* samsara

lower scope. First of the three levels of *lamrim* practice: lower, medium, and great. *See* ten nonvirtuous actions

mahasiddha (Sanskrit; great yogi). Accomplished tantric *yogi*.

Mahayana (Sanskrit; Great Vehicle). The teachings of the *Buddha* that lead to the accomplishment of *bodhichitta* and eventually, in combination with *wisdom*, to *enlightenment*; includes *Paramitayana* and *tantra*.

mala (Sanskrit). Rosary of usually 108 beads used to count recitations of *mantras*.

mandala (Sanskrit). Deity's mandala; the residence of the *buddhas,* depicted differently for each. *See also* mandala offering *and* Kalachakra mandala *in Mantras and Practices*

mantra. Sanskrit syllables representing various qualities of the *buddhas,* such as compassion and *wisdom,* that are recited in order to create *merit,* purify negative *karma,* get rid of problems, heal illness, and, finally, to lead to *enlightenment. See Mantras and Practices for various mantras*

merit. Positive qualities; virtue; good karmic imprints.

method and wisdom. The two aspects of the path to enlightenment, the *lamrim.* Method is associated with compassion and the altruistic actions of a *bodhisattva; wisdom* is associated with ridding the mind of *delusions,* accomplished in the first stages of the *lamrim,* and, finally, the realization of *emptiness.*

mudra (Sanskrit; seal). A symbolic hand gesture used in certain practices.

naga (Sanskrit; serpent). Snakelike beings with human intelligence—usually not visible to humans—who live in or near bodies of water and who, like spirits, can often cause harm. *See also* naga incense pujas and naga torma *in Mantras and Practices*

nirvana. *See* liberation

omniscience. *See* buddha

Padmasambhava. Guru Rinpoche; eighth-century Indian master who helped bring Buddhism to Tibet. *See also* Guru Rinpoche prayer to clear away obstacles *in Mantras and Practices*

Paramitayana (Sanskrit; Perfection Vehicle). The first of the two *Mahayana* levels of practice, the other being *Tantra Vehicle.*

path to enlightenment. *See* lamrim

perfect complete wisdom, perfect complete compassion, perfect complete power. *See* buddha

puja (Sanskrit; offering). Usually used to refer to a ritual, such as the *Guru Puja,* or the reciting of a *sadhana. See also* Guru Puja merit field *in Mantras and Practices*

pure land. *See* Amitabha Buddha's pure land

rebirth. *See* reincarnation

reiki healing. A Japanese healing technique that works on the body's subtle energies.

reincarnation. Rebirth; the Buddhist teaching that soon after death, the mind of every *sentient being* leaves that life and takes another birth within *samsara,* determined by their *karma.*

renunciation. The wish to give up suffering and the causes of suffering because of the conviction that there is nothing worthwhile in *samsara;* the accomplishment of the first two stages of *lamrim* practice.

retreat. A period of time, from a few days to several years, taken out of day-to-day life for meditation and *Dharma* practice.

sadhana (Sanskrit). The practice of visualizing oneself as a *deity* and reciting various prayers and *mantras.*

samsara (Sanskrit). *Sentient beings* are "in samsara" because of possessing *delusions* and creating *karma,* and thus are compelled to take rebirth again and again in the various realms. There are the three realms (form, formless, and desire); and, in turn, the desire realm is divided into six (upper realms: *deva, asura,* human; lower realms: animal, *hungry ghost, hell*).

Sangha (Sanskrit). Spiritual community; monks and nuns; ordained ones; the third of the three objects of refuge: *Buddha, Dharma,* and Sangha. *See also* refuge *in Mantras and Practices*

self-cherishing. Selfishness; putting our own needs before the needs of others; the main obstacle to the achievement of *bodhichitta.*

sentient beings. In Tibetan, "mind-possessors"; unenlightened beings in the various realms of *samsara.*

sexual misconduct. One of the *ten nonvirtuous actions;* commonly refers to adultery.

Shantideva. Eighth-century Indian monk-saint; wrote *A Guide to the Bodhisattva's Way of Life.*

six realms. *See* samsara

spirit harm. Harm done by spirits to *sentient beings* by possessing them or making them ill.

stupa (Sanskrit). Buddhist reliquary, ranging in size from huge to a few inches in height and representing *omniscience.*

subtle mind and body. In tantra, one of the three levels of a person's physical and mental energies, *gross,* subtle, and *very subtle.* The subtle body consists of the channels, *winds,* and drops; the subtle mind, accessed only by accomplished meditators, can cognize phenomena not congized by the gross mind: the past and future, the minds of others, etc.

sutra (Sanskrit). A discourse of the Buddha; a Buddhist teaching that is not *tantra.*

tangka (Tibetan). Religious painting.

tantra (Sanskrit). Buddhism's esoteric teachings, part of the *Mahayana;* a text that describes the tantric teachings.

Tantra Vehicle (Sanskrit: *Tantrayana*). *See* tantra

ten nonvirtuous actions. Refraining from these ten is the main practice of the *lower scope* of the *lamrim:* killing, stealing, sexual misconduct, lying, divisive speech, mindless chatter, harsh speech, covetousness, malice, and holding wrong views.

three higher trainings. The practices of morality, *concentration*, and *wisdom. See* four noble truths

three realms. *See* samsara

transmigratory being. *See* sentient being

two truths. Ultimate truth (*emptiness)* and conventional truth (all other phenomena).

Universal Education School, Bodhgaya. A school in India affiliated with the *FPMT* whose curriculum is based on Buddhist principles but is outside the religious context. (Universal Education is now known as Essential Education; essential-education.org.)

upper realms. *See* samsara

Vasubandhu. See *Abhidharmakosha*

wind. According to *tantra,* one of the components of the subtle body of *sentient beings,* along with channels, chakras, and drops. The winds course through the thousands of channels, including the *central channel,* along with the various states of mind that they are associated with, such as *attachment.*

wind imbalance (Tibetan: *lung*). According to Tibetan medicine, an imbalance of the *winds* manifests as the various illnesses.

wisdom. Accomplished gradually as one removes *delusions* from the mind, realizes *emptiness,* and, finally, attains omniscience.

yogi. An accomplished tantric meditator.

Mantras and Practices

..... *Included here are brief explanations of all the practices mentioned by Rinpoche in this book, as well as many of the actual mantras. All terms in italic in the entries below can be found as their own entry here or in the Glossary. The practices themselves and the mantras can be found on fpmt.org/DLZ.*

Amitayus. Along with White Tara and Namgyelma, one of the three *buddhas* mainly associated with long life.

OM AMARANI JIVAN TIYE SVAHA

Black Court Case mantra.

OM NAMO BHAGAVATE / ARHATE SAMYAKSAM BUDDHAYA / TADYATA / OM MUNI MUNI / MAHA MULANA / RAKSHA SARVA PUSHTIM KURU SARVA / TATAGATA / ADISHTANA ADISHTADE / NAMA SARVA RAKYA RAKYA SVAHA

OM KATUM RAKYA / OM KACHU SÖD TRARAKYA / OM NI WARA SUNRAKYA HARA HARA RAKYA RAKYA SVAHA

TADYATA / OM VAJRAPANI MAMA RAKYA RAKYA / OM JODO / KACHU MARAYA PHET / SAMAYA TU RAKYA / HUM HUM PHET PHET SVAHA

Black Garuda. A practice for healing illness, especially cancer.

Black Manjushri. A wrathful aspect of the Buddha of Wisdom.

OM TRA SÖ / CHU SÖ / DURTA SÖ / TURMI SÖ / NYINGOLA CHÖ / KHALA JA / KAM SHAM TRAM BÄ PHET SVAHA

bodhisattva vows. One of the sets of *three vows*, belonging to the *Mahayana* level of practice; commitments, taken by lay and ordained people for life, to use one's life for the benefit of others.

buddhas of the ten directions.
From *The Sutra Illuminating the Darkness of the Ten Directions:*
East: Tathagata, arhat, perfectly completed buddha Following Deeds.
South: Tathagata, arhat, perfectly completed buddha First Mentally Generating, Many Aspects of Beauty to the Mind, Free of Fear and Panic, the Clearly Superior King.
West: Tathagata, arhat, perfectly completed buddha Subduing Malice and Arrogance.
North: Tathagata, arhat, perfectly completed buddha Placed with a Jewelled Body of Radiant Light.
Northeast: Tathagata, arhat, perfectly completed buddha Subduing and Destroying All Demons and Indecision.
Southeast: Tathagata, arhat, perfectly completed buddha First Generating Mind, Having the Glory of Irreversible Wheel.
Southwest: Tathagata, arhat, perfectly completed buddha of Jewelled Parasol with Superior Radiance.
Northwest: Tathagata, arhat, perfectly completed buddha Subduing Bodhisattvas.
Above: Tathagata, arhat, perfectly completed buddha the Clearly Superior King of Concentration Without Fear and Free of Darkness.
Below: Tathagata, arhat, perfectly completed buddha Living and Abiding in Cutting Off Doubt and Agitating Afflictions.

calm abiding meditation (Sanskrit: *shamata*; Tibetan: *shiné*). A type of meditation that enables one to access subtler, more refined levels of one's mind and to eventually develop single-pointed concentration, which allows one to cut through *delusions*, realize *emptiness*, and get out of *samsara*.

Chenrezig. The Buddha of Compassion.

SHORT MANTRA
OM MANI PADME HUM

MEDIUM-LENGTH MANTRA
NAMO RATNA TRAYAYA / NAMA ARYA JÑANA
SAGARE / VAIROCHANA VYUHA RAJAYA
TATAGATAYA ARHATE SAMYAK SAMBUDDHAYA /
NAMA SARVA TATAGATEBHYAH ARHATEBHYAH
SAMYAK SAMBUDDHEBHYAH / NAMA ARYA
AVALOKITESHVARAYA BODHISATTVAYA
MAHASATTVAYA MAHAKARUNIKAYA / TADYATA /
OM DHARA DHARA DHIRI DHIRI DHURU DHURU
ITTI VATTE CHALE CHALE PRACHALE PRACHALE
KUSUME KUSUME VARE / ILI MILI CHITI JVALAM
APANAYE SVAHA

chetrul puja. Method to get rid of an evil spell.

circumambulation. Practice of walking clockwise
around a holy object, such as a *stupa,* as a
method for accumulating *merit.*

Compassion Buddha. *See* Chenrezig

death and impermanence. In order to energize
oneself to want to practice *Dharma,* it's
recommended in the *lamrim* to meditate on the
fact of impermanence, that everything changes,
in the context of one's own death: specifically
that (1) death is definite; (2) the time of death is
uncertain; and (3) all that counts at the time of
death are the karmic imprints left in the mind
from one's practice of virtue.

Diamond Cutter Sutra. One of the shorter *sutras*
on *wisdom.*

dream yoga. Tantric *yogis* use the subtle mental
experience of the dream state for spiritual
practice.

eight Mahayana precepts. A set of vows taken for
twenty-four hours: no killing, lying, stealing,
sexual activity, eating after noon, listening to
music, wearing jewelry, sitting on high seats.
See also three vows

Exalted King of the Mantra of the Great Breath.
TADYATA / DARA DARA / DA DARA DA DARA /
TARA TARA / TA TARA TA TARA / MARA MARA
/ MAMARA MAMARA / HU DHU HU / HA HA HA
/ SARA SARA SARA / CHU CHU CHU / BU BU BU
/ KILI KILI KILI / SARVA BHUTA / ADHIPATI /
DRA DRA DRA / BRA BRA BRA / KHU KHU KHU
/ KRA KRA KRA / YASA YASA YASA / PANDARE
PANDARE PANDARE / HULU HULU HULU / HU
HU HU / DAGLA SUNGSHIG SUNGSHIG [MAY I BE
PROTECTED] / CHILI CHILI CHILI / MILI MILI MILI
/ KSHO KSHO KSHO / GAURI GAURI GAURI / DAGGI
NETAM CHERAB TUZHI BARGYUR CHIG [MAY
ALL MY SICKNESS BE COMPLETELY PACIFIED]
SVAHA / MAHA SHVESA SVAHA / MAHA BHUTA /
ADHIPATAYE SVAHA / GAURYE SVAHA / UGRAYA
SVAHA / DAG DELEG SUGYUR CHIG [MAY
I BECOME HAPPY AND GOOD] / DAM KSHATRI
KARALA PIMGALA AJNYA PAYATE SVAHA

five lay vows. A set of *pratimoksha,* or individual
liberation, vows: No killing, lying, stealing,
sexual misconduct, or alcohol and drugs. *See
also* three vows

**Five Powerful Mantras for Liberating Sentient
Beings from the Lower Realms.**

1. KUNRIG (VAIROCHANA)
OM NAMO BHAGAVATE / SARVA DURGATE
SHODHANI RAJAYA / TATAGATAYA / ARHATE
SAMYAKSAM BUDDHAYA / TADYATA / OM
SHODHANI SHODHANI / SARVA PAPAM
BISHODHANI / SHUDHE BISHUDHE / SARVA
KARMA AVARANA VISHODHANI SVAHA

2. MITRUGPA (AKSHOBHYA)
NAMO RATNA TRAYAYA / OM KAMKANI
KAMKANI / ROCHANI ROCHANI / TROTANI
TROTANI / TRASANI TRASANI / PRATIHANA
PRATIHANA / SARVA KARMA / PARAM PARA NI
ME / SARVA SATTVA NANCHA SVAHA

3. *NAMGYELMA (USHNISHAVIJAYA)*
Om bhrum svaha / om amrita ayur da de svaha
At the conclusion, recite:
Om amrite amritotbhave / amita vikrante / amita gate / amrita gamini / amrita ayur da te / gagana kritti kare / sarva klesha kshayam kariye svaha

4. *STAINLESS PINNACLE (USHNISHAVIMALA)*
Nama treya dhikanam / sarva tatagata hri daya garbhe jvala jvala / dharma dhatu garbhe sambhara mama ayu samshodhaya / mama sarva papam sarva tatagata santoshnisha vimale vishuddhe hum hum hum hum / am bam sam ja svaha

5. *WISH-GRANTING WHEEL*
Om padmo ushnisha vimale hum phet

Foundation of All Good Qualities. A short *lamrim* verse text by *Lama Tsongkhapa.*

four powers for collecting merit. Four factors that determine the power of one's virtuous deeds: (1) the power of the attitude, the best being *bodhichitta;* (2) the power of the object, the most powerful being the *guru;* (3) the power of vows, creating virtue in the context of keeping vows; (4) the power of phenomena: in terms of giving, the giving of *Dharma* creates the most extensive *merit.*

Green Tara. *See* Tara

Guru Rinpoche prayer to clear away obstacles.
See also Padmasambhava *in Glossary*

Precious Guru, the embodiment of all buddhas of the three times;
Great Bliss, the lord of all accomplishments;
Wrathful Power, the one who dispels all hindrances and subdues demons;
Pray bestow you blessings.

Please remove the outer, inner, and secret obstacles, and
Grant your blessings to accomplish wishes spontaneously.

Guru Puja merit field. The array of *holy beings* that one prays to while reciting the tantric practice, *Guru Puja* (Tibetan: *Lama Chöpa;* English: *Offering to the Guru*).

Heart Sutra. A teaching of the Buddha on *emptiness* that contains the following mantra.
Tadyata [om] gate gate paragate parasamgate bodhi svaha

highest yoga tantra initiation. Permission to practice a deity within the highest of the four classes of *tantra.*

hundred-torma offering. A practice for accumulating *merit.*

inner-offering pills. A type of blessed pill used in tantric practice.

Jambhala (Tibetan: Dzambhala). A *buddha* associated with the generation of wealth. Rinpoche usually recommends the practice of Yellow Jambhala.
Om jambhala jalandraye svaha

Kalachakra mandala. Abode of the *buddha* Kalachakra, often drawn with colored sand.

Kshitigarbha. A *bodhisattva* renowned for his compassionate wish to save beings from the *lower realms.*
Tadyata muni more / muni gha be / muni ki li dha ye / muni rogi ba tsa le / muni hali de / muni gha me she bha khye / mirla bhag / khe bha la la bhag khye / so ri kir ta / tor na kir tsa le / bha tag sha kir te / ku ku la mir le / ava shya sa re / er ha ki li bha / muni bha thaba svaha

lamrim prayer. See *Foundation of All Good Qualities*

light offerings. Offerings of candles and other lights; may be put on one's altar, offered extensively at a holy site, or visualized.

Lion-face Dakini. Female *buddha* whose practice counteracts spirit harm and other negative influences.

AH KA SA MA RA / TSA SHA DA RA / SA MA RA YA PHET

Logyönma. A female *buddha* for purifying obstacles and disease.

lu puja. A puja done to counteract harm from *nagas*.

Maitreya Buddha. The next Buddha to come to this world, after *Shakyamuni Buddha*.

MANTRA OF MAITREYA BUDDHA'S PROMISE
NAMO RATNA TRAYAYA / NAMO BHAGAVATE SHAKYAMUNIYE / TATAGATAYA / ARHATE SAMYAKSAM BUDDHAYA / TADYATA / OM AJITE AJITE APARAJITE / AJITAÑCHAYA HA RA HA RA MAITRI AVALOKITE KARA KARA MAHA SAMAYA SIDDHI BHARA BHARA MAHA BODHI MANDA BIJA SMARA SMARA AH SMA KAM SAMAYA BODHI BODHI MAHA BODHI SVAHA

HEART MANTRA
OM MOHI MOHI MAHA MOHI SVAHA

CLOSE-HEART MANTRA
OM MUNI MUNI SMARA SVAHA

mandala offering. A visualization of the universe according to Buddhist cosmology and the recitation of the components of the universe, offered to the *buddhas*.

Mantra Purifying All Negative Karma and Defilements.

OM BI PULA GARBHE MANI PRABHE / TATAGATA DHARI SHANI / MANI MANI SUPRABHE VIMALA SANGARA GAMBHIRA HUM HUM JVALA JVALA / BUDDHA VILOKITE GUHYA / ADHISHTITE GARBHE SVAHA / PADMA DHARA AMOGA JAYATI CHURU CHURU SVAHA

Marichi. Female *buddha* for pacificying external obstacles.

OM MARICHIYE MAM SVAHA

Medicine Buddha. Pujas are done to the seven Medicine Buddhas plus *Shakyamuni Buddha*, or to the main Medicine Buddha alone, to overcome illness, life hindrances, and other obstacles to success.

MANTRA FOR THE MAIN MEDICINE BUDDHA
TADYATHA / OM BHAISHAJYE BHAISHAJYE MAHA BHAISHAJYE [BHAISHAJYE] / RAJA SAMUDGATE SVAHA

Medicine Buddha name mantra.
To the bhagavan, tathagata, arhat, fully enlightened buddha, Medicine Guru, King of Lapis Light, I prostrate, make offering, and go for refuge.

Milarepa. Tibetan eleventh-century meditator and saint, renowned for his devotion to his *guru*, attainment of *enlightenment* in his lifetime, and his many songs of spiritual realization.

OM AH GURU HASA VAJRA SARVA SIDDHI PHALA HUM

Most Secret Hayagriva. A wrathful *buddha* of compassion.

naga incense puja and **naga torma.** Offerings of (1) incense and (2) a special kind of cake to *nagas*.

Namgyelma. Along with Amitayus and White Tara, one of the three *buddhas* mainly associated with long life. (For mantra, *see* Five Powerful Mantras.)

nyungné (Tibetan). Two-day fasting and purification practice focusing on the *buddha Chenrezig*, including prayer, meditation, and prostrations.

One Who Gazes with a Compassionate Eye. *See* Chenrezig

powa pill. A blessed pill put on the crown of a dying person to help the consciousness take a good rebirth when it leaves the body at death.

pratimoksha vows (Sanskrit; individual liberation vows). One of the sets of *three vows*; includes various sets, including the *five lay vows* and the vows of monks and nuns that belong to the *Lesser Vehicle* level of practice, and which are lifelong. The five main vows for monks and nuns are similar to the vows for lay people, except that monks and nuns take a vow of celibacy.

preliminary practices. Various practices, such as *water bowls* and *mandala offerings*, that are performed 100,000 times as a "preliminary" practice to entering tantric *retreat*.

printing texts and mantras. The practice of making copies of scriptures and holy words.

prostrations. An elaborate "bow" that involves prostrating oneself on the floor. Traditionally the way to greet one's *guru* or done before sitting down to meditate, hear teachings, etc. Hundreds of thousands of prostrations are also done as a *preliminary practice*.

protection cord. Blessed amulet or cord usually worn around the neck to protect the wearer from various types of obstacle.

refuge. The practice of relying on, taking refuge in, the *Buddha* and his *Dharma* and *Sangha* as the basis of one's spiritual practice, starting with the wish to stop creating negative *karma*, the first stage of the *lamrim*.

Shakyamuni Buddha. The buddha whose teachings are practiced at this time in history, born in India 2,500 years ago.

Tadyata om mune mune maha muneye svaha

Six Yogas of Naropa. A set of tantric practices, including *dream yoga, powa*, and inner fire, associated with the Indian master Naropa.

Stainless Pinnacle. *See* Five Powerful Mantras

sur offering. The practice of offering the smell of burning barley flour and butter to the *hungry ghosts*.

Sutra of Golden Light. Rinpoche recommends that this *sutra* be recited to help stop violence and war.

Tangtong Gyelpo. Fifteenth-century Tibetan yogi who composed *Prayer Liberating Sakya From Disease,* which helps remedy epidemics, and *Prayer for Preventing War.*

tantric vows. One of the sets of three vows, taken by people who have received a *highest yoga tantra initiation.*

Tara. A female buddha; the practice of Green Tara is popular among Tibetan Buddhists, for success in worldly and spiritual activities.

Om tare tuttare ture svaha

Short Tara prayer
Om I prostrate to the goddess foe destroyer,
   liberating lady Tara,
Homage to tare, savioress, heroine,
With tuttare dispelling all fears,
Granting all benefits with ture,
To her with sound svaha I bow!

tea offering prayer. *Ablution to the Eight Worldly Powerful Spirits.*

Thirty-five Buddhas of the *Sutra of Three Heaps.* These are the central figures in a practice of visualizing the *buddhas,* who vowed to help *sentient beings* purify their negative *karma,* and reciting their names, followed by a confession prayer.

thought transformation (Tibetan: *lojong*). Mind training; a series of methods for developing *bodhichitta* that includes cherishing others more than oneself, accomplished through the practice of *tonglen.*

three vows. Groups of various vows according to the different levels of practice: *pratimoksha, bodhisattva,* and tantric. *See* five lay vows

tonglen (Tibetan; giving and taking). Exchanging oneself for others; the *Mahayana* practice of taking on *sentient beings'* suffering and giving them one's happiness, done in formal meditation using one's breath: breathing in the suffering of others and taking it upon oneself and breathing out one's own happiness and giving it to them.

tsatsa (Tibetan). A small statue of a *buddha* or other holy object made out of plaster or some similar material from a mold.

Vajra Armor (Tibetan: *Dorje Gotrab*). A practice for removing obstacles and curing illness.

Om pema shawa re hung peh / nen par shig / naga nen / ta ya ta / sawa / be re ta / hana hana / vajra na / raja raja / soha

After reciting the mantra, blow on water, then drink or apply to skin; or blow on cream or butter and apply. In your daily practice, after you finish reciting the mantra, hold your hand in front of your mouth, then blow air upward into your nostrils.

Vajrapani Hayagriva Garuda. A practice of visualizing these three *buddhas* together in one form; for protection.

Om vajrapani hayagriva garuda hum phet

Vajrasattva. A practice done especially for purfication.

HUNDRED-SYLLABLE MANTRA
Om vajrasattva samaya manupalaya / vajrasattva tvenopatishta / dridho me bhava / suposhyo me bhava / sutoshyo me bhava / anurakto me bhava / sarva siddhim me prayaccha / sarva karma su chame / chittam shriyam kuru hum / ha ha ha ha ho / bhagavan sarva tatagata / vajrasattva ma me muncha / vajra bhava maha samaya sattva ah hum phet

SHORT MANTRA
Om vajrasattva hum

Vajrayogini. Female *buddha* who represents purified attachment.

wealth vase. A container filled with precious things and blessed substances that helps the practitioner enhance wealth.

Wheel of Sharp Weapons. A text by tenth-century master Dharmarakshita that describes the process of *karma.*

water-bowl offering. Offering bowls of water as a practice of purification and creating *merit;* one of the nine *preliminary practices* of the Gelug tradition of Tibetan Buddhism that are performed 100,000 times. *See* preliminary practices

White Umbrella Deity. A female *buddha* who protects from the dangers of the elements.

Tadyata om anale anale vishade vishade vaira vaira vajradhari bandhani bandhani hum hum phet phet svaha

Wisdom Publications

Wisdom Publications, a not-for-profit publisher, is dedicated to making available authentic Buddhist works for the benefit of all. We publish translations of the sutras and tantras, commentaries and teachings of past and contemporary Buddhist masters, and original works by the world's leading Buddhist scholars. We publish our titles with an appreciation of Buddhism as a living philosophy and with the special commitment to preserve and transmit important works from all the major Buddhist traditions. If you would like more information or a copy of our mail-order catalog, please contact us at:

Wisdom Publications, 199 Elm Street, Somerville MA 02144, USA
Telephone: (617) 776-7416 • Fax: (617) 776-7841
Email: info@wisdompubs.org • www.wisdompubs.org

The Lama Yeshe Wisdom Archive

The Lama Yeshe Wisdom Archive is the repository of the teachings of the late Lama Thubten Yeshe and his heart-disciple, Lama Thubten Zopa Rinpoche. The Archive collects the audio recordings of these teachings and transcribes and edits them for trade publication, for the Web, and for free distribution in booklets, including the latest booklet by Lama Zopa Rinpoche, *The Joy of Compassion*. If you would like copies of these free booklets, or if you would like to support the mission of the Archive, which is ongoing, please visit the Website or contact the Archive directly.

The Lama Yeshe Wisdom Archive, PO Box 356, Weston MA 02493, USA
Telephone: (781) 259-4466 • Fax: (678) 868-4806
Email: info@lamayeshe.com • www.lamayeshe.com